AFRICAN AMERICAN ARCHITECTS

Embracing Culture and Building Urban Communities

Melvin L. Mitchell
Author of *The Crisis of the African American Architect*

African American Architects
Embracing Culture and Building Urban Communities

Publication and editorial management of this book was by Katherine Williams, a registered architect and former editor of NOMA MAGAZINE, 2009-2014.

Graphic design of the book and front cover was by Lou Moriconi, The indexer was Virginia Ling.

The National Museum of African American History and Culture cover photograph (left side) is courtesy of the Smithsonian Institution-NMAAHC. The right side photograph of the Bridge Park development in Dublin, Ohio is courtesy of Moody/Nolan, Inc.

Library of Congress control number: 2020901013

ISBN: 978-1-7344960-0-0

For Geraldine.
You made all of my fondest hopes and dreams come true.

Contents

INTRODUCTION

Whose Architects "Will Tell Our Story"?
...And Help Us to Rebuild Our Communities?

This book, *African American Architects: Embracing Culture and Building Urban Communities*, is the sequel to *The Crisis of the African American Architect: Conflicting Cultures of Architecture & (Black) Power,* my first published book in 2002. *The Crisis* was 400 pages of small text, footnotes, and no photographs or graphic images. My target audience was the professional and academic wings of the African American architect community. The title was indeed my central thesis.

African American Architects: Embracing Culture and Building Urban Communities has a much smaller amount of text, larger fonts, more than 200 pictures and illustrations, and no academic footnotes. My intent is to expand my initial target audience to include the cross section of people shown in the photograph below. Those are the people typically found queuing daily in front of the new National Museum of African American History & Culture (NMAAHC) on the National Mall in Washington, DC since its grand opening in September 2016. A majority are black, but clearly there are many others of every race, religion, creed, color and nationality. Their increasing curiosities now encompass architecture, African American architects, and the cultural cross connections of both to their own lives and identities.

The book's main front cover photo, left side, shows a partial view of the NMAAHC building set against the 172-year-old Washington Monument. Not a single one

I.1 American citizens in line awaiting entrance to the NMAAHC, ca. 2018. Source: Author

of the other five competing finalist designs could have even remotely provided the same timeless and visually compelling counterpoint to that monument.

The architects for the NMAAHC project on the book cover, top left to right are the late J. Max Bond, Jr. (1935-2009), the literal dean of the nation's black architects over the last thirty years of his career up until his death in 2009; Phil Freelon (1953-2019), a full generation younger than Bond, but someone who fulfilled his early promise of becoming Bond's heir apparent (Freelon died in July of 2019 after a three year battle with ALS disease); Zena Howard, a woman, who is nearly a generation younger than Freelon, played a vitally important role in the design and building of the NMAAHC project. Her presence speaks volumes about the essentiality of black women in architecture.

I.2 NMAAHC winning submission, Freelon Adjaye Bond/Smith Group. Source: Courtesy of Smithsonian-NMAAHC

Next is David Adjaye, a generational cohort of Howard. Adjaye was born on the sub-Saharan African mainland, raised in Ghana, and trained in England. Adjaye completes the diasporic connection that was a vital factor in this African American and African architect consortium's design of the now globally iconic NMAAHC structure.

The fifth architect on the book cover is Curtis Moody. Though not a member of the NMAAHC design team, Moody's firm, Moody/Nolan Inc. is currently the nation's indisputably premier black-owned architectural engineering firm. Moody/Nolan is also consistently ranked as one of the top fifty architectural firms in the nation. Moody's firm is the lead designer and Architect of Record for the large urban hous-

I.3 NMAAHC finalist renderings. 1. Antoine Predock-*Moody/Nolan, Inc.*; 2. Diller Scofidio+Renfro; 3. Norman Foster-URS. 4. Moshe Safdie-*Sulton Campbell Britt;* 5. Pei Cobb Freed-*Devrouax+Purnell* (African American architects names in italics) Source: Slate Magazine, ca 2009

ing development shown in the right-frame of the cover photo. This Columbus, Ohio-area project, containing nearly 1,000 housing units, hotels, and one million square of office-retail space, is just a small testament to the enormous capacity of the Moody/Nolan firm.

The two projects provide a representative example of the potential and capability of today's African American architect practitioner corps in two critical arenas; culture-civic design, in the case of the NMAAHC project, and housing and community development in the case of the Moody/Nolan firm's Bridge Park project. Over the coming decade black-founded and owned architectural firms must pursue both types of projects. However, there must be a one-hundred-fold increase in the latter type and with the architect as initiating and financial risk-taking entrepreneur.

The NMAAHC project has brought about a dramatically positive change to the image of African American architects in the eyes and minds of Black America, and the world at large. Going forward, the prospects and opportunities are without bounds. *But only if…;* and I identify those ifs throughout the final half of this book.

This book was precipitated by my mid-2017 re-reading of three of the key books that instigated my writing of *Crisis* twenty years ago. Architect–professor Roger K. Lewis's *Architect? A Candid Guide to the Profession* is a well-meaning book by a principled and justifiably acclaimed architect-educator. I find Lewis to be exasperatingly misguided and simplistic in his assumptions about the cultural neutrality of architectural school preparation.

In a similar vein, architectural historian Carter Wiseman's now twenty year-old opus, *Shaping a Nation: Twentieth Century American Architecture and Its Makers*, is a book that continues to bemuse (more so than enrage) me for its glaringly shallow understanding and portrayal of the actual shaping of American culture over the past two centuries.

I.4 Book Cover.
Source: Author

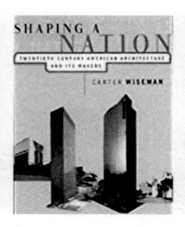

I.5 Book Cover.
Source: Author

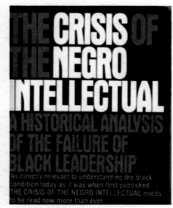

I.6 Book Cover.
Source: Author

The third book is Harold Cruse's now fifty-year-old magisterial tour de force, *The Crisis of the Negro Intellectual: A Historical Analysis of the Failure of Black Leadership*. Cruse's book continues to be my North Star. Cruse reminded us of the reality of the American social, economic, and cultural construct as a *nation of groups* despite the focus of the U.S. Constitution on the *individual*. For me Cruse now more than ever substantiates the reality and necessity of a Black America that acts on its own *group economic* interests.

Each of the nation's groups is a representative slice of a pie. One of the main groups is Black America. At the end of 2018, that group comprised forty-four million people, a thirteen percent slice of the pie. In theory, though clearly not always in deed, every single *individual* African American within the group is fully protected by the U.S. Constitution. Yet African Americans as a *group* lag woefully behind the other main groups; mainly WASPS, other non-black ethnics, and Jewish Americans. African Americans as a group lag in all critical measures of relative group economic well-being.

I continue my argument that there is a direct correlation between Black America's seemingly intractable and unacceptably low levels of home, property and business ownership and net wealth as a *group* – and Black America's thus far failure to collectively re-engage in physically building things, particularly shelter, housing, communities, and even new cities. Black architects may not be responsible for this but today they possess the possibility of moving to the forefront of Black America's dire need to start building things.

The already globally iconic NMAAHC structure may represent the dawn of a renaissance era for twenty-first century African American architects, a largely invisible group of people in America prior to September 2016. But I hasten to add that the NMAAHC could also represent the sun setting on African American architects as business-owning professional practitioners who actually take on the liabilities and responsibilities of making and building things.

The overall number of black licensed architects will continue to grow, but the number of independent architect-practitioner entities in the United States is on track to decline to a statistical zero over the coming generation. Equally alarming is that this trend tracks remarkably well with Black America's group decline in family home ownership and net worth. Reversing both of these trends require that a new generation of African American architect–practitioners join hands with Black America in a new *movement* to *actually build* millions of new houses and homes in dozens of urban–suburban centers across the nation that are currently under assault by urban gentrification.

The 1999 *Encyclopedia of the African and Africana: The Encyclopedia of African and African American Experience* edited by Henry Louis Gates and a star-studded collection of scholars profiled over 2,000 individuals . Those profiles were put forth by Gates et. al. as the quintessential representatives of black culture production across the African diaspora. Gates and his scholars did not list or profile a single African American or African architect. The 2016 opening of the NMAAHC building has changed *everything*.

I argued in my first book in 2002 and continue that argument today that the year 1892 was a fateful starting point in the twentieth century struggle of Black America's fledgling corps of architects. That year the young American Republic unveiled plans to open to the public the following year a grand celebratory exposition to display to the rest of the world its industrial and technological might and know-how as a white Christian civilization.

The Columbian Exposition, also known more commonly as the Chicago World's Fair, opened May 1, 1893 on 600-acres of land on Chicago's south shore. Chicago's all-white civic, government, and business organizers called upon America's most prominent architects and landscape architects to provide the physical manifestation of the celebration of the 400th anniversary of the discovery of America by Christopher Columbus.

The World's Fair organizers had a predictable attitude toward the nation's four million black people, then only twenty-eight years out of chattel slavery.   Meaningful and positive black representation in the World's Fair was largely prohibited. The only exceptions allowed were for exhibits that emphasized the primitive and exotic. The collateral intent of the fair organizers was further debasement of the black race. Black America's leadership observed this with proper alarm. One of those observers was thirty-six-year-old Booker T. Washington, head of the fledgling Tuskegee Institute in Alabama. Washington believed that he could, through the use of stealth and deception, counter the White City. He set about the building of what he believed was a necessary black equivalent   on the grounds of Tuskegee Institute just six hundred miles south of Chicago.

Washington launched his counter-quest with the recruitment of Robert R. Taylor, Black America's first formally educated architect. Taylor graduated in mid-1892 from Massachusetts Institute of Technology (MIT). By that time, the Tuskegee campus had expanded beyond the 100-acre chicken farm acquired by Wash-

I.7. The Court of Honor, Chicago World's Fair, ca. 1893. Source: Wikipedia Commons

I.8. Tuskegee Normal & Agriculture Institute, Tuskegee Alabama, ca. 1916.
Source: Wikipedia Commons

ington in 1881. Here, black architects were afforded the chance to build big buildings approaching the scale of Chicago's World's Fair buildings.

In 2002, the year I published *Crisis,* I went ahead with my plan to voluntarily retire as director of the Institute of Architecture and Planning (now the School of Architecture & Planning) at Morgan State University in Baltimore. After five very personally fulfilling years I left in order to pursue another passion; in 2003 I became an active member of the National Organization of Minority Architects (NOMA). I also resumed my dormant professional practice as well as part-time adjunct teaching in the still fledgling architecture program at the University of the District of Columbia (UDC).

I.9 African American Architect Magazine cover Spring 2004. Source: Author

In that same year the gavel of NOMA leadership was passing to president-elect James Washington of New Orleans. This very accomplished architect was taking over an organization that had fallen on difficult times over the prior several years. Membership was down, finances were in disarray, and the NOMA image—its brand, if you will—was, at best, murky. Washington had a bold plan to fix all of those things. He eventually succeeded spectacularly. Today's completely revived, revamped, and rapidly growing NOMA owes a huge debt of gratitude to him.

My first move as an active NOMA member was to transform the NOMA monthly newsletter, a four-page, letter-sized pamphlet with black and white low-resolution photos. That newsletter had been in existence since NOMA's founding in 1971. My objective was a full-color quarterly magazine printed on high-quality glossy paper. I was determined that the magazine's name should be *African American Architect*. Others in NOMA felt strongly that the name should be *NOMA Magazine*. The inaugural issue debuted in spring 2004 under the compromise name of AFRICAN AMERICAN ARCHITECT: *Magazine of the National Organization of Minority Architects*. The theme of that issue was "The Black Culture Museum: Expressing the African American Spirit Through Architecture."

Utmost in my mind was the acute awareness that the decades-old plan for the ultimate black museum on the National Mall in Washington, DC was clearing one hurdle after another and could soon become a reality. We were all acutely aware of the prevailing etiquette for architect selection. Only A-list architects would be invited to submit qualifications for a project of the magnitude of the planned NMAAHC project. No black-owned firm would even make the short list of finalist firms to be interviewed to design such a project. Ensuring that an African American architect–led team would design this museum was the number one priority of NOMA in 2003.

I also used my article and the entire magazine issue to highlight several other large black-themed museums. In 2012 Columbia University architecture professor Mabel Wilson released the definitive book on the past one hundred years of collective black struggle to build a museum of national culture on the National Mall. Wilson's *Negro Building: Black Americans in the World of Fairs and Museums* began with the 1895 Atlanta Cotton States and International Exposition and traced the movement right up to the final version of the Charles H. Wright

I.10 Howard Simms.
Source: Courtesy of Jack Travis

I.11 Harold Varner.
Source: Courtesy of Jack Travis

I.12 Charles Wright Museum of African American History, Detroit, ca. 2001.
Source: Wikipedia Commons

Museum of African American History that opened in Detroit in 1997. The Wright museum architects Howard Simms (1934–2016), and Harold Varner (1935–2013) were profiled in the 1991 Jack Travis book, *African American Architects in Current Practice.*

The Wright Museum was by far the largest of the black museums. The design was an unapologetically Afrocentric approach that sought to distinguish itself from the heroic modernist tropes and themes that dominated architecture prior to the 1970s' post-modernist period. Varner stated that his use of a grand rotunda interior and numerous exterior devices was inspired by his travels through West Africa.

Upon Varner's death in 2013, the firm continued under Howard Simms as SDG Associates. Simms died in 2016 after a lengthy illness. SDG continues under the leadership of a second generation of architect-managers. The firm continues its longstanding role as one of Detroit's most influential practices; it has helped to shape the face of the city while training scores of black architects.

Walter Blackburn (1938–2004) and his wife, Alpha Blackburn first proposed their Indianapolis-based architecture firm's design for the National Underground Railroad Freedom Center project in 1994. The project broke ground in 2002 and opened in 2004. The project overtook the Wright Museum in Detroit as the largest of all of the black museums. The Howard University-trained couple put forth a design that was heroic modernist with bare hints of Afrocentrism. The project's location on the banks of the Ohio River

I.13 Walter Blackburn, I.14 Alpha Blackburn.
Source: Wikipedia Commons

I.15 Underground Railroad Freedom Center, Cincinnati, Ohio, ca 1998.
Source: Wikipedia Commons

in downtown Cincinnati offers the possibility of becoming a transformative urban economic development despite its still non-urban setting.

I used the magazine cover, the main article and several color photos to sing the praises of very capable young Raleigh-Durham architect Phil Freelon. I saw Freelon as being a serious alternative to Max Bond if need be. Freelon had completed a dozen black-themed museums around the country. In 2004, he was overseeing the construction completion of his superb Reginald F. Lewis Maryland Museum of African American History & Culture (MMAAHC).

I had become aware of Freelon and his palpable talent in 1997 during my first year as director of the Morgan State University architecture program. That year, I was also a mayoral appointee to the influential Baltimore Design Review Committee. We were charged with reviewing and approving all new building design proposals in the city. Sitting at the top of our long list of projects to be reviewed and voted on was a proposed revision to a twice-rejected earlier proposal to the design review committee. The project was the long-awaited Reginald Lewis MMAAHC project.

The design review panel was unanimous in its disapproval of the newest revision by the initial architects. Full Maryland state funding was in place but under threat of being rescinded unless an approved design was advanced. The review panel concluded that it was time to dismiss the current architectural team and start anew. I put forth the suggestion that we invite Bond and another former Howard classmate, Gary Bowden, who was a senior vice president of RTKL, Baltimore's

I.16 Gary Bowden and Phil Freelon ca 2000. Source: Author

I.17. The Reginald Lewis MMAAHC, ca. 2004. Source: Author.

largest architectural firm. Each man was invited to submit a statement of interests and qualifications. Bond was too busy at that time and did not respond.

But Bowden was very much interested. Bowden, sensitive to the racial-political dynamics of Baltimore, relayed to me his intent to team his big (white) firm with a capable young black firm. I pointedly suggested to Bowden that he call Freelon.

The call was made, and the two of them jointly submitted a statement of qualifications proposal for the Maryland museum project. The Bowden/Freelon oral presentation of their conceptual ideas was made to a joint Baltimore city and state design review panel. Their presentation left everyone on the joint panel momentarily speechless. There was unanimous approval that we had the team and the concept for the new museum.

In that 2004 inaugural *African American Architect* NOMA magazine issue, I did something that I thought at the time was unrelated to the looming NMAAHC issue. I inserted a short article with the cryptic title "Who Is David Adjaye?" I provided an accompanying photo of Adjaye that I took from the cover of the March 2004 issue of AZURE Magazine.

We were convinced of the need for a selection process that required each finalist team "to tell the story" of Black America and the black experience. We believed that these two factors would level the playing field and add immeasurably to the chances that Black America's best and brightest architects would be shortlisted and eventually selected.

Looking back now, it is highly likely that the NMAAHC museum director, Lonnie Bunch, was already of the same mindset, however he arrived there. By 2006, Bond and Freelon, obviously seeing each other as serious contenders for what would be the design commission of the twenty-first century, decided to join forces rather than each pursue the NMAAHC project as competitors. Fortuitously, the Smithsonian decided to request proposals from architects to prepare pre-design studies for the project. The Freelon/Bond team submitted a proposal and was able to win that contract.

This was a brilliant piece of positioning strategy by Bond and Freelon. In 2008, the Smithsonian announced an international design competition. By then, David Adjaye had been in the United States for several years, designing daring new public libraries in Washington, DC, while also winning several large, prestigious international design competitions. Adjaye had also been watching events unfolding for the NMAAHC project. Predictably, Adjaye had long been an intense admirer of Bond and his illustrious career. Adjaye called Bond and Freelon to express his interest in teaming with them to pursue the project.

Bond and Freelon were both aware that Adjaye by that time was the most high-profile black architect on the planet. Word has it that the three met in a New York City coffee house and found that the chemistry between them was excellent. The Freelon/Bond decision to expand the team to include Adjaye may have been the most insightful stroke-of-genius move of the century.

Some have long wrestled with the idea of an Afrocentric architecture in America. My problem with the Afrocentrist camp was their overt use of non-sub-Saharan African motifs and images. The 4500-year-old pharaonic-era Egypt and its stone temples and pyramids were their preferred source of architectural imagery and motifs. History may ultimately vindicate such Afrocentrist ideas. Having studied and read extensively on the subject, I remain an agnostic.

I have been more interested in the documented African American lineage to the West African region of today's nation states of Senegal, Sierra Leone, Liberia, Ivory Coast, Ghana, Togo, Liberia , Ghana, and Nigeria. Among a dozen tribes, the dominant culture is Yoruba. I have been long intrigued by the prospect that there might have been important things of an art and architectural nature happening in that part of the world between 600 BC and 1200 AD. I suspected that those things may have been as consequential as the art and architecture of Europe between 500 BC and 1200 AD.

Enter David Adjaye, born in Tanzania in 1966 to Ghanaian parents and trained in

I.18 David Adjaye, ca 2017. Source: Wikipedia Commons

I.19 Olowe sculpture.
Photo source: Wikipedia Commons

I-20. The exterior metal panels, and I.21. Washington Monument cap angles, and NMAAHC corona angles. Photo sources: NMAAHC/Alan Karchner

England. Freelon and Bond entrusted Adjaye with the role of lead design architect of the NMAAHC project. Adjaye's inspired choice of using imagery and motifs
drawn directly from the West Africa–Yoruba culture for the main building of the
NMAAHC was accepted enthusiastically by Freelon and Bond. Adjaye's inspiration for the building's form was drawn from a sculpture by Nigerian artist Olowe
of Ise.

Borrowing directly from Adjaye's description, the exterior of this structure,
whose frames lean outward to create the thin screen or "scrim" perforated by
geometrical   patterns based on historic iron grilles found in African American
communities in Charleston, South Carolina, and New Orleans. The original design proposed that the scrim be made of bronze, which would have made the
museum the only one on the National Mall whose exterior was not made of lime-
stone or marble.

These decisions were counter to the classical European architecture on the mall.
The NMAAHC architecture is a deft fusion of West African and African American craftsmanship, art, and architecture by a West African and African American
team of architects. The juxtaposition of the NMAAHC corona (or crown-like tiers)
angles with the angle of the top cap of the 172-year-old Washington Monument
is Adjaye's insightfully pointing out the link between these two African architectures.

Max Bond had worked with his FAB team members (and the Smith Group for production drawings and specifications) right up to the time of the design's submission in late 2008. Tragically, Bond died two months before the April 2009 architect-selection decision was made. Just weeks before the Smithsonian selection
panel would announce its choice of the architect team to design the NMAAHC,
very influential people in the world of architecture were making known their own
choices. During that time, conversations with Lonnie Bunch, the NMAAHC director and a member of the selection panel, yielded no clues. Bunch was diplomat-
ically unreadable. The influential *Washington Post* architecture critic, Ben Forgey,
devoted his entire column to advocating for the one short-listed proposal that I
thought was the absolute worst possible design. A number of other people whose
opinions I held in high regard were deeply opposed to the Freelon Adjaye Bond
proposal. I was astounded that there were people that were not seeing what I was
seeing.

Throughout the NOMA family, we were heartened by the knowledge that—just as
we had all lobbied so hard for—the ten-person Smithsonian architect-selection
panel was a stellar collection of citizens with a racial composition that did not
look like the prior typical architect-selection panels for big signature buildings.

Before the actual selection of the finalist architect team the mood of trepidation
was best captured by the words of Steve Lewis, the son of an accomplished retired
architect. Lewis—an AIA Fellow, Whitney Young award winner, long-time professional
practice owner, and currently a partner at ZGF, a large majority owned architectural firm—was the sitting president of the National Organization of Minority Architects
(NOMA). He was speaking through the vehicle of *NOMA Magazine*, the successor to
the *African American Architect* magazine that I had started in 2004 .

Lewis took over editorial and publishing responsibilities in 2006 and propelled the magazine to quality and content heights that exceeded my fondest hopes as well as my technical capacities. Here were his words in the days right after the April 14, 2009, selection announcement:

> After anxiously awaiting the Smithsonian Institution's selection of the architect for the highly competed National Museum of African American History & Culture, members of NOMA released one giant, collective sigh of relief with the announcement by museum director Lonnie Bunch of the Freelon Group, with David Adjaye, Davis Brody Bond, and the Smith Group as the winning team.

I.22 Steve Lewis. Source: Courtesy of Steve Lewis.

Lewis went on to explain the reasons behind that "collective sigh of relief":

> For African American architects, the emotions leading up to the announcement were disturbingly reminiscent of the doubts and fears that so many of us felt on the eve of the nation's 2008 presidential election night. Could, or would such an important commission be awarded to a black architect?

Lewis went on to the heart of the source of the anxiety:

> People need to understand why this is so important to so many within the Black community [Black America]. For almost 400 years we have endured the telling of our history by others… On Tuesday, April 14, 2009, the question of "who will tell our story" was put to rest.

The black architect–designed museums movement reached a crescendo with the September 2016 opening of the NMAAHC. African American architects now have the attention of Black America and much of the rest of the world. So, what is to be done with this attention? Many more museums and other structures celebrating black culture are still needed. Most certainly those efforts must continue. The continuation of the designing and building of those museums and other culture-preserving edifices are a necessary fact of life for Black America. Equally important is the immediate need by Black America of the kinds of projects that will directly impact the gaps in Black America's oft-cited low indices of comparative family net worth, home ownership, and business creation.

In September of 2018, NMAAHC curator Michelle Joan Wilkinson organized a three-day symposium titled "Shifting the Landscape: Black Architects and Planners, 1968 to Now." Wilkinson's choice of the year 1968 in the title of her symposium was very appropriate. That was the year of Dr. King's assassination. Yet more to the point of the symposium, 1968 was the year of a now widely known speech delivered by the National Urban League head, Whitney Young, Jr., to a virtually all-white gathering of the nation's architects at their annual American Institute of Architects convention in Portland, Oregon.

From September 27-29, 2018 Wilkinson assembled inside of the NMAAHC structure a virtual who's who lineup of the nation's African American architect- practitioners, architect-academics, and an assortment of community planning-design activists. For three full days, there were speeches, panel discussions, debates, and other forms of discourse. The objective was to salute the nation's black architects while also undertaking an assessment of the previous fifty years through the exchange of ideas about the coming decades for the nation's black architects and urban planners. The fellowship and comradery in that NMAAHC gathering was high.

Wilkinson and the NMAAHC provided the nation's black architects and planners a huge spotlight of visibility. No overarching message was offered by the architects to each other and the students in attendance about *next steps*. Rather, the message appeared to me to be, *"Go back to your home turfs and double down on what you are now doing."* It is likely that there could have been no other outcome, given the symposium's format and limited timespan.

I would argue that the seeds of *next steps* for the symposium participants can be found in two places; the first place should come from a drilling down on Whitney Young's 1968 speech—actually the keynote address (www.aia.org) in Portland. For Young, nearly everybody can quote the "your thunderous silence and complete irrelevance" money-shot line from his lengthy speech delivered to a stony-faced, virtually all-white audience of architects. However few people are actually aware of the full social, economic, and political content and depth of the speech. Even fewer know anything at all about the person, Whitney Young, Jr.

Young, a major organizer of the 1963 Martin Luther King, Jr.-led March on Washington, was the president of the National Urban League from 1961-1971. Under Young's leadership, the National Urban League became the black radical organization of its day for much of middle-class Black America. Closer to my premise

I.23 Whitney Young, Jr. ca 1970. Source: Wikipedia Commons

here, it was Young who first floated the idea of a domestic Marshall Plan for those American cities that had large black populations living in what were universally referred to as ghettos.

The fact that stands out most of all is how Young's successor, Vernon Jordan, at Young's prodding, issued the first annual "National Urban League State of Black America Report" in 1972. The NUL-SoBAR tradition is now in its forty-fifth year. Over the past decade, under the leadership of former New Orleans mayor Marc Morial, the SoBAR has continued to take on increasing significance as a consensus measurement of the relative state of the health and welfare of Black America. Just as important, the NUL has revived its push for a domestic Marshall Plan.

The late twentieth-century information technology revolution has completely disrupted the 150-year-old business model for the architecture profession. While there will continue to be exceptions, twenty-first-century architect-practitioners are being compelled to adopt business models that completely integrate the silos of development, finance, design, fabrication, sustainable and resilient construction, costs, energy consumption, and occupancy maintenance. Ironically, a close approximation of such a fully integrated model prevailed during the building of Tuskegee Institute in Alabama one hundred-years ago.

Between the years of the Great Depression (1920s to 1940s) and today, a major failure of national black leadership has been its inability or unwillingness to develop a black-dominated shelter and housing industry in America. The need to establish a degree of hegemony in the development and building of housing for a significant portion of Black America—as well as for other Americans in need—would have been enormously difficult to do in post-reconstruction America. However, the building of Tuskegee Institute during a reign of white state- sanctioned terrorism against black citizens is evidence that this was not an impossibility.

There is a long overdue need for a movement to create a housing industry in Black America. Today the objective of such a movement should be a ten-year plan to build at least one million affordable houses in gentrifying communities in urban areas across America. Instigation, agitation, and a leadership in such a movement would be the African American architects' equivalent of a moonshot on behalf of Black America.

However again, this will require that a large breakaway segment abandon the architecture profession's still prevailing cultural orthodoxy. That deeply ingrained orthodoxy views housing as being "not really architecture…it's something builders and developers do."

The lingering overriding perception that black architects are not yet viewed as being *essential* in the manner of black doctors and black lawyers can be dramatically changed. The place to start would be by declaring and demonstrating to Black America that black architects can be counted on as ardent and effective advocates in the battle to ensure that the necessary houses, homes, and vibrant community environments will be provided. In a word, black architects as a group must demonstrate to Black America that they are about something far bigger than their own professional interests as narrowly defined by architecture profession and academic orthodoxy.

PART I of this book is a highly truncated and pictorially supplemented personal perspective on the period from pre-Christian antiquity through the first half of the twentieth century. The small group of African American architects of this first half of the twentieth century designed buildings that left indelible marks and footprints over the course of the twentieth and early twenty-first centuries. Those buildings have been totally unacknowledged in the mainstream print media, and have also been poorly promoted in black print media.

PART II begins with my part-personal and abbreviated rough draft memoir and is followed by my several interpretive essays on the closing decades of the twentieth century. I have been privileged to live through all of the second half of the twentieth century. I personally experienced the second coming of black political power in the 1960s (the first coming was during the 1867-1877 Reconstruction era). Black architects began to see some respite from some of the first half-century race-based obstacles.

However, just a single generation into that second half of the twentieth century saw the onset of the information technology revolution that proved to be a very different nemesis. This set of obstacles has been far more daunting than white racism. The internet, globalization, the digitization and speed-of-light travel of all data including inert matter, and artificial intelligence (AI) have caused the total disruption of all businesses and business models. The negative effects of fossil-fuel usage on the environment and climate add further challenges for the entire African diaspora.

PART III is where I offer what I believe are imperatives for an awakening group of architects of all races and genders who are prepared to break ranks with twentieth century architectural orthodoxy. Though not enough and not fast enough, there are growing numbers who are already are doing so.

PART I

ARCHITECTS AND BLACK AMERICA 1900–1950

"Whites wont hire you, and blacks can't afford you."

– A high school teacher to
teenager Paul R. Williams, ca. 1910

---

1. Global Antiquity to Post-Reconstruction in America

A brief survey of how architecture is discussed and written about in mainstream culture might be a useful guide to the general reader. A cautionary note is in order. The consensus view of architectural historians should not be confused with the views of regular academic historians. Consensus architectural history marks the 10,000-years-ago point of fixed settlements and rudimentary building structures as the beginning of architecture. Such settlements and structures began appearing in the Tigris -Euphrates River Valley in Mesopotamia, which is also known as the Cradle of Civilization. This era marked the ending of the Ice Age and hunter–gatherer movement. This was the period of transition to societies based around agriculture and animal husbandry. Ironically, today's nation-state of Iraq occupies the geographic center of this part of the world.

Fast-forward from 8000 BC to 500 BC in Greece, also known as the golden age of Western civilization. The architectural icon for that period is the Greek Acropolis, with the Parthenon as the main building.

Things move rapidly from the Greece of purist and exacting visual aesthetics across the Aegean Sea to the Italy and Imperial Rome of 1AD. The Romans conquered Greece and absorbed Greek civilization. They transformed Greek architecture by adding bold engineering to transport water, sewage, people, and goods. The dominant master builder-architect of that period was Vitruvius, whose description of architecture—firm, commodious, and delightful—is still regarded as *the* definition of architecture.

1.1. Map of The Middle East today. Source: Wikipedia Commons

1.2. The Parthenon on the Acropolis, Athens, Greece constructed ca. 500 BC.
Source: Wikipedia Commons

After showing numerous additional 500 BC to 300 AD slides of Greek and Roman building types to my history students, I could always count on looks of awe on their faces. After letting those moments settle in, I would then inform them that I had several more slides to show from a time 1,000 years earlier, in Egypt, located in northeast Africa.

Without fail, after showing a few slides like these there would be a barrage of questions that led to intense discussion and debate. I always closed my slide lecture by suggesting that my students read *Black Athena: The Afroasiatic Roots of Classical Civilization, Vols. I & II*, by Martin Bernal, a respected British scholar and retired Cornell University professor. Bernal released the first volume in

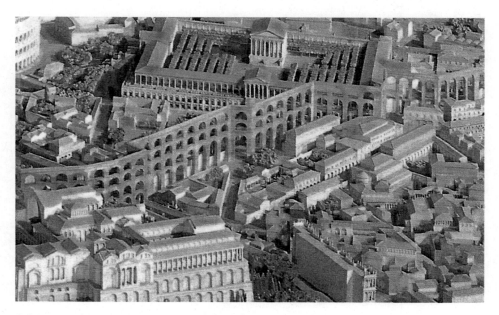

1.3. Imperial Rome AD 1. Source: Wikipedia Commons

1.4. Mortuary temple of Queen Hatshepsut in Deir el-Bahari, Egypt constructed ca 1500 B.C.
Photo source: Eye Ubiquitous / Alamy Stock

1987. I also steer my students to several other scholars, such as Mary R. Lefkowitz, co-editor of *Not Out of Africa: How Afrocentrism Became an Excuse to Teach Myth as History, Black Athena Revisited* (1996), with Guy MacLean Rogers, her colleague at Wellesley College. In that book, the ideas of Martin Bernal are further scrutinized by another respected classics scholar who fiercely rebuts Bernal's thesis. I advise them to read both books and make up their own minds.

The period between AD 1, the embrace of Christianity, and the fall of Rome in AD 300 was followed by a period generally referred to as the "Middle Ages"

I.5 St. Peter's Basilica and Square, Rome. Completed 1626 AD.
Source: Wikipedia Commons

I.6 The Great Mosque of Diene, Mali West Africa ca 1907, a mud brick structure originally built in the 13th century and rebuilt constantly. Source: Wikipedia Commons

or "Dark Ages." When discussing the thirteenth and fourteenth centuries, great emphasis was placed on having architecture students learn to identify pictures of the plans and perspective views of the magnificent soaring Gothic cathedral structures by name. The cathedrals, however, are conceded to be the works of obscure "master (stone mason) builders" rather than architects.

In architecture school we jump ahead from Rome around the time of the birth of Christ to the fifteenth century Italian Renaissance, which is acknowledged as a rebirth of Imperial Rome that spanned from 400 BC to 400 AD. The subject of the architecture of West African empires and cultures from 1 AD to the fifteenth century just never arose. With a few exceptions, West African structures were not built with stone, brick, or other materials capable of lasting hundreds of years.

Accordingly, the western civilization mindset did not view African structures as qualifying as architecture (Egypt and its monumental stone architecture was not perceived as being in Africa while I was in architecture school during the 1960s). Wilson Jeremiah Moses brings great clarity and depth to this subject in his engrossing book *Afrotopia: The Roots of African American Popular History (1998).*

Architecture school history books spend some time on the period between the end of the Italian Renaissance and the mid-eighteenth-century onset of the Industrial Revolution in the British Isles. This revolution began around 1750 AD, over 9,000 years after the Agricultural Revolution in Mesopotamia.

I am constantly reminding students and young faculty that unconditional hero worship of early twentieth century modern architects is misplaced. The real heroes were the nineteenth century scientists, engineers, and inventors. The real accomplishments are the marvelous practical applications of science and technology these men (and a few women) brought to bear in the buildings generated by the Industrial Revolution.

Architectural historians tend to obscure the projects and people that provided

1.7. The Crystal Palace, London completed ca. 1851. Source: Wikipedia Commons

1.8 The Eiffel Tower, Paris, France. Completed 1889.
Source: Wikipedia Commons

us with, for instance, the solutions to the materials and technical knowledge of skeletal steel frames that made high-rise buildings possible. Without such engineering and technically devised framing materials and techniques, there could be no high-rise structures for architects to wrap wall-type curtain skins around. Bridge-building engineers satisfied real needs for incredibly large spans via their creative use of steel or concrete. This also provided the tools and techniques that would allow architects to build with artistry that extended beyond purely practical considerations. Far too little attention is directed to, for instance, the Great Exhibition of 1851, better known as the Crystal Palace of London. This one-million-square-foot structure of cast iron-framed, glass-enclosed exhibition space rivals the magnificent soaring railroad stations of Europe. The designer, Joseph Paxton, was neither an architect nor an engineer.

No high-rise building is of the slightest practical value without the key features of the Eiffel Tower of the Paris World Exhibition of 1889. To build the Eiffel Tower engineer Gustave Eiffel had to rely on two previous inventions: the transformation of iron ore into high-strength carbon steel, and the elevator, created by engineer-inventor Elisha Otis in 1852. High-strength reinforced concrete is another engineering breakthrough that allowed our early twentieth century modernist architect heroes to claim original authorship of amazing structures.

It is impossible to imagine the modern world as we know it without engineers and scientists. Yet a plausible case can be made that *beauty*—the commodity that architects contend is their real expertise and contribution—would still be present in an all engineer–scientist world.

People who made no clear distinctions between themselves as builders, engineers, or architects have created beauty throughout the ages. A more objective architectural history that is still to be written in the twenty-first century will show that the modern European and American architect icons of the early twentieth century were more propagandists and brilliant self-serving publicists than critical innovators. The new history may show that engineers and scientists were the real heroes we should be enshrining. For the next generation of African American architects, a much deeper review of the true contributions of 19th and early twentieth century engineers and scientists must be a first order of business.

The last 2,500 years of the 10,000-year history of architecture must be written as a more honest depiction of the pervasive black suppression and the feigned invisibility of black achievement and black impact. The next order of business is for deeper reviews of the influence of Cubist art and Negro jazz and blues music on modern architecture. This will only happen through new realizations throughout Black America that presumptively *white* modern architecture can be no whiter than today's American music, dance, and other cultural art forms.

2. Booker T. Washington
Creates America's Black Architects, 1892–1915

> *"I must study politics and war, that my sons may have the liberty to study mathematics and philosophy. My sons ought to study mathematics and philosophy and geography, natural history, and naval architecture, navigation, commerce, and agriculture in order to give their children the right to study painting, poetry, music, and architecture."*
>
> —John Adams, ca. 1700

A consensus exists throughout mainstream white academic and professional American architecture that Thomas Jefferson (1743-1826) is the ultimate father figure for the nation's architects. At the end of the eighteenth century, Jefferson was at a transitional point in his life as a political theorist, gentleman architect, and owner of nearly two hundred mostly American born African slaves.

Jefferson spent his post-William and Mary College life pursuing his architectural ambitions and education through reading and practicing the drawing rules of the École des Beaux-Arts, the Paris-based authority on all matters of architecture in the Western world at that time. His 1780s stay in Paris heightened his architectural aspirations.

From his political writings and recorded utterances, we know a great deal about his innermost thoughts. Jefferson expressed grave misgivings about the intellectual capacities of the slaves in his home state of Virginia. We also know that Jefferson's slave and mistress Sally Hemings bore sons for Jefferson and that at least one of the sons was trained on the plantation as a carpenter. We know that Jefferson would have found the idea of a full-blooded African (someone of no known or obvious evidence of white parentage) capable of being educated and socialized as an architect—as Jefferson understood that term—to be highly improbable. We can only speculate on how Jefferson would have felt about the prospects of a mulatto, quadroon, or even octoroon slave becoming an architect.

Virtually any slave—undiluted blood line or otherwise—that Thomas Jefferson might have chosen to mentor and publicly acknowledge as his architectural protégée would have very likely gone down in history as one of America's most revered architects with fountainhead status. Had Jefferson, for instance, chosen to send his carpenter son to the École des Beaux-Arts with full acknowledgment, that act would have had a profound impact on the historical image of the African American architect throughout the nineteenth and twentieth centuries.

By the mid-1800s, white American architects were emulating Thomas Jefferson by traveling to Paris. Richard Morris Hunt was the first American architect who would go on to achieve icon status after making the trek to Paris.

Hunt studied at the École des Beaux-Arts in 1855 before returning to America to

2.1 Booker T. Washington

2.2 Thomas Jefferson.
Sources: Wikipedia Commons

train others in his atelier. Several African American scholars have written about Lewis Metoyer, an American man of color in Paris who received architectural training at the Ecole in 1875. Metoyer's father was French, and his mother was a black slave in Louisiana. Metoyer returned home to Louisiana to build in the nineteenth century.

Frank Lloyd Wright, who would become the leading figure in the American architecture world, was born in 1865. In that same year, a nine-year-old Booker T. Washington was emancipated from slavery and was within sixteen years of founding Tuskegee Institute shortly after graduating from the industrial education program at Hampton Institute in Virginia. Meanwhile, outstanding white American architects were serving the titans of this country's mushrooming industries. The burgeoning architects were designing factories, office buildings, and grand estates created from the great personal fortunes of new American industrialists.

William Ware, one of William Morris Hunt's students, established the first American architecture school at the Massachusetts Institute of Technology (MIT) in 1865. The curriculum was patterned after the École des Beaux-Arts. However, Black Americans would have to wait nearly twenty years to see a black person accepted into the MIT program.

Booker T. Washington (1856-1915), unlike Thomas Jefferson, did not actually study architecture or fancy himself as an architect. However, Washington was resolute that a professional architect's skills were needed in order to carry out his vision for Tuskegee.

Like most visionaries, Washington appreciated the end product of architecture. He was in awe of what he regarded as a profound cognitive developmental and conceptualization process that went into the making of the drawings for architecture.

2.3. Tuskegee Institute, and the 100-acre chicken farm acquired in 1881.
Source: Wikipedia Commons

Washington was well aware of the white supremacist convictions of Thomas Jefferson in building the University of Virginia in 1819. But several scholars believe that Washington was emulating Jefferson in the belief that architecture was essential to the building of Tuskegee in Alabama.

Washington exhausted all of his resources developing the first rudimentary campus structures during the first nine years after founding Tuskegee in 1881.

2.4. University of Virginia yard and academic village core, ca. 1825.
Source: Wikipedia Commons

He passionately believed that it was essential that he create full-fledged architects—in addition to carpenters and bricklayers. In Washington's mind, the African American architect–practitioners he created at Tuskegee were the synthesis of what would eventually become known as the Washington–DuBois debate.

Tragically, standing squarely in the way of Washington's ambitious plans was a venal white-power ethic that was aptly characterized by Supreme Court Justice Roger B. Taney's infamous Dred Scott dictum: "The Negro has no rights that a white man is bound to honor."

Mr. Washington believed that the principal role of the African American architect should be that of a change agent and catalytic instrument of black economic and community development on a land base. Conversely, we have to surmise that his nemesis, the W.E.B. DuBois turn-of-the-twentieth-century era thinking about the necessity of a black land base and a "black economy" was conflicted. DuBois was rightly convinced that without the vote, civil rights, and social equality, black land holdings and black economies were hopelessly vulnerable to white caprice.

Washington and DuBois each operated from a completely different geographic and political arena. One harbored a specific goal-oriented agenda of constructing a physically rooted institution. The other was about a grand idea of political consciousness, struggle, and resistance. Several modern historians have posited that there was indeed a joint understanding and coordinated strategy between Washington and DuBois. Clearly, both men were right. In retrospect, it is hard to conceive that there was no silently understood middle-ground strategy between them. The simplicity of conventional thinking about Washington is made apparent through a careful reading of August Meier's *Negro Thought in America* (1963). There are also Washington's own words at the Atlanta Cotton States Exhibition in 1895, and Mr. DuBois's critique of Washington in that familiar chapter, "On Mr. Washington and Others," in his acclaimed book *The Souls of Black Folk* (1903).

By 1900, the 100-acre farm and scattered chicken shacks that Washington had acquired from the Alabama legislature in 1881 had grown considerably. By then, there was an at least 1,000-acre campus with many substantial buildings and over 1,200 students. Washington never posited the original Tuskegee as a college. He saw it as a vocational school that would prepare some people to go on to prestigious colleges for final training and return to Tuskegee and other industrial schools. Washington was apparently willing to serve as a useful straw man to the very necessary urgings of W.E.B. DuBois for classical university education for the creation of a "Talented Tenth" in Black America.

That 1890–1920 period is best symbolized by a combination of seminal architectural events that would also define American architectural culture. The 1893 Chicago World's Fair of monumental European Beaux-Arts architecture that so captivated the country's ruling elites was one such event. Better known as the Columbian Exposition, this fair was the physical centerpiece of the observance of the 400th anniversary of Christopher Columbus's 1492 landing in the "new world."

The event was also intended to showcase the United States as a world power. Frederick Law Olmstead, designer of Central Park in New York City and the

2.5. Bird's eye view of the 633-acre Chicago World Columbian Exposition, 1893.
Source: Wikipedia Commons

father of American landscape architecture, was tasked with laying out the fairgrounds. Daniel Burnham, the influential Chicago architect, was the executive charged with the responsibility of selecting the various architects for the World's Fair buildings. The opening words of Burnham's famous and often quoted dictum, "Make no little plans…. for they fail to stir the hearts of men," captured the spirit of the twentieth century at its beginning.

Burnham idealized the midwestern business men who would become the captains of industry and commerce. Another less often quoted statement by Burnham even better sums up the dreams of America's architectural leaders. His desire was to serve the personal wealth and burgeoning corporate and industrial ambitions of the virtually all-white world of American business. Burnham can be paraphrased this way: "I want to build a big organization that can do big things for big businesses…."

The architecture profession was, as was everything else in American civilization, a whites-only proposition. The very term *African American architect* was an oxymoron. In 1892, Frank Lloyd Wright, destined to become the most famous architect in modern history, was a rising young draftsman in the Chicago office of Louis Sullivan.

A group of black citizens, led by Ida B. Wells and Frederick Douglass, lobbied hard to gain an opportunity and place at the 1893 fair that would display black progress. The only black presence allowed at the fair were exhibits that were

2.6. The Court of Honor and Liberal Arts Building, 1893 World's Fair.
Source: Wikipedia Commons

exotic, backward, and a further debasement of over four million black people.

Booker T. Washington was watching the unfolding Chicago Fair from his perch at Tuskegee as he struggled in the white terrorist state of Alabama. His Don Quixote–like dream in 1881 was morphing into a bigger dream to transform that initially 100-acre chicken farm into a "Black City" architectural equivalent of the "White City" of the Chicago World's Fair.

In 1892, Washington took a fateful step toward actualizing his ambitions. That year, Robert Robinson Taylor (1868-1942) graduated from the architecture program at MIT in Cambridge, Massachusetts. He was the first of his race to enter the program in its twenty-five year existence. Taylor, the son of a successful North Carolina builder, was the valedictorian of his MIT class. Taylor's successful progress at MIT was not going unnoticed by Booker T. Washington and his wide-ranging circle of confidants.

Whether Taylor had to be coaxed back to the Deep South and Tuskegee or saw this prospect as the opportunity of a lifetime is conjectural. What is certain is that Washington felt that Taylor personified the perfect blend of the Washington-DuBois debate on the education of Black America in the post-slavery era. Taylor possessed formal exposure to classic aspects of Western civilization as well as the practical hands-on skills and knowledge to design and manage the construction of a building of any size or function.

Mr. Washington, had the difficult task of casting two different faces. The first face

2.7 Robert R. Taylor at age 21.
Source: Wikipedia Commons

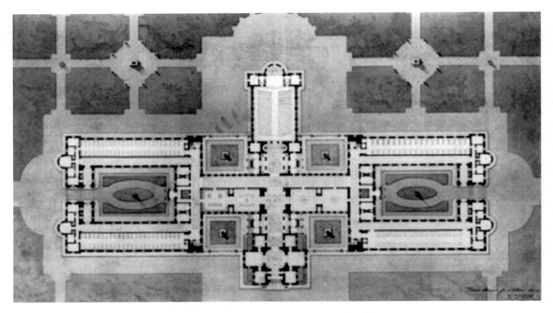

2.8 Taylor's 1892 MIT Thesis floor plan for a home for retired soldiers.
Source: Wikipedia Commons

2.9 Taylor's Thesis main elevation drawings. Source: Wikipedia Commons

was to the local white population. That face had to uphold the idea that at Tuskegee he was only training vocational trade craftsmen. Many people to this day assume that such craftsmen and trade mechanics were the only logical products that could have resulted from Washington's educational, social, and economic enterprise at Tuskegee Institute.

Washington's success in bringing Taylor to Tuskegee in 1892 was the stroke of insightful action that eventually afforded African American architects the opportunity to pursue Daniel Burnham–type architectural dreams of designing and building big 1893 Chicago World's Fair–type buildings. This reality must be contrasted with Washington's standing before the Atlanta Cotton States Exhibition in 1895 and giving his famous accommodation speech, declaring that his only interest was in leading a "not yet civilized Negro people" to become the trader-laborer base for a "new" (white-led) South. Washington was playing a much bigger and stealthier long-range game that in his mind required telling whites what they wanted to hear from black leaders.

Thanks to the doctoral dissertation of black architect-scholar Richard Dozier, (University of Michigan, 1990) and a book, *Robert R. Taylor and Tuskegee: An African American Architect Designs for Booker T. Washington (2012)* by Tulane University professor Ellen Weiss, we know much about the first architects Mr. Washington recruited to Tuskegee between 1881 and 1915. Washington's hidden face was that of architect Robert Taylor and other African American architects

2.10. Tuskegee Institute vocational shop class, ca. 1892. Source: Wikipedia Commons

he recruited to Tuskegee. Such men and their most talented students focused on the design and building opportunities available at the developing Tuskegee campus and within black communities spread about the Deep South and the southeastern seacoast.

Booker T. Washington's dream of economically self-controlled black communities could only be partially and sporadically achieved. Yet, in spite of the rigidly imposed caste and racial system of his time, Mr. Washington's architects in black communities were often at the center of such successes. Contemporary African American architects and their practices are direct physical and spiritual descendants of those architects deliberately hand-picked 125 years ago by the much-maligned Mr. Washington.

Washington passionately believed that it was essential to create full-fledged architects in tandem with his loudly trumpeted commitment to creating carpenters and bricklayers. Washington viewed the actual design and construction management of his "Black City" in the heart of the Alabama black belt as something too important to be contracted out to the white architects and builders that so many of the wealthy white industrialist-philanthropists tried to attach to their financial gifts to Tuskegee for large buildings.

Washington's architects mastered the same architectural design rules, principles, canon, vocabulary, and technology used by the nation's white architects. However, they were building structures on the Tuskegee campus and through-

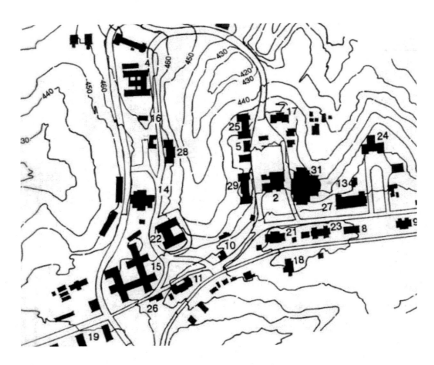

2.11. A 1910 map of nearly 30 buildings dotting Tuskegee's 1,500-acre campus as Washington's counter to the 1893 Chicago World's Fair. Source: Wikipedia Commons

out the Deep South for the use of powerless, illiterate, and often penniless ex-slaves seeking to transform themselves into a modern people. All of this was taking place under the cruelest conditions and within an unrelenting form of racial apartheid.

After Taylor's arrival in 1892, the faculty and students jointly achieved levels of self-sufficiency in the design and construction of the Tuskegee campus that are breathtaking in retrospect. They constructed a brick-making plant that provided all of their bricks, and lumber mills for wood. They developed and built all of their own hoisting and heavy materials–moving mechanisms. Here was comprehensive, fully integrated, environmentally balanced land development, design-build construction management, and critical materials manufacturing in one entity. The scope and magnitude mirrored the best large-scale commercial and industrial efforts occurring then in white America.

Washington evolved a clear modus operandi in developing his scores of campus buildings, farm structures, and an adjacent residential community of homes for Tuskegee faculty and administrators. His endeavor, driven by his architect faculty and students, entailed acquiring hundreds of acres of virgin farmland in the midst of a hostile and violent Alabama.

The early twentieth-century South had no black leisure class. The several extant black industrialists and real estate developers were far too few and isolated to build on a scale anywhere nearing that of Mr. Washington's Tuskegee campus.

2.12. Thrasher Hall completed in 1893. Source: Wikipedia Commons

2.13 The Oaks, Booker T. Washington Residence completed in 1900.
Source: Wikipedia Commons

2.14 Huntington Hall, completed 1899. Source: Wikipedia Commons

2.15 White Hall, completed in 1909. Source: Wikipedia Commons

2.16 Tomkins Hall, completed 1910. Source: Phillip Scolia, Alamy Stock Photo

His architect-builder teachers and those they trained went forth throughout the Deep South to build black churches, Jewish philanthropy–funded schools, an occasional business place, and private residences for the few who could afford them.

With the exception of Tompkins Hall the above representative sampling of Tuskegee buildings completed between Taylor's 1892 arrival and Washington's death in 1915 were mostly all *signature buildings* designed at Tuskegee and throughout southern black communities by Mr. Washington's early twentieth-century black architects (Tompkins Hall was designed by a white Atlanta architect with Taylor providing complete construction management of the project). These buildings represent a classic example of architecture and architects that have remained invisible. This work is largely unheralded to this day on the larger American stage of twentieth-century architecture.

Mixed feelings throughout Black America about Mr. Washington range from loathing to indifference. The post-Booker T. Washington generation of African American architects has had limited success in establishing architecture in the minds of African Americans as a vital, relevant, and *essential* component of black life in a way that is similar to the place held by medicine and law.

Thus, we have in bold relief the two simultaneously occurring seminal architectural events in Black America and white America in the final decade of the nineteenth century. For white America, it was the 633-acre, multi-million-dollar world-exposure extravaganza along the downtown Chicago lakeshore. For Black America, it was a 100-acre farm being transformed into a 2,000-acre, multi-building institutional campus in the middle of the violently racist Alabama black belt.

Only the former event is unfailingly featured in standard architecture textbooks

2.17 The Tuskegee Chapel, 1897. Source: Wikipedia Commons

2.18 Robert R. Taylor
at age 38 in 1906.
Source: Wikipedia Commons

2.19 Philip A. Payton.
Source: Wikipedia Commons

2.20 W.E.B. DuBois.
Source: Wikipedia Commons

as a serious architectural accomplishment. The latter event is, predictably, of no interest or relevance to mainstream architectural historians and media. What was not so predictable was that the latter event would be treated so lightly by Black America's intellectual and academic leadership.

The Tuskegee campus and surrounding community subdivisions are still today, 125 years after the 1892 arrival of Taylor, the largest private real estate assemblage and new development deal ever put together inside of Black America. This accomplishment was achieved by an all-black cast of characters dominated by trained African American architects and builders.

Interestingly, Mr. Washington, from his base at Tuskegee in the first decade of the twentieth century, was also instrumental in abetting another large-scale, black-conceived and executed real estate deal. Ample documentation shows Washington's indirect financial and political sponsorship of men like Philip A. Payton, Jr. (1876-1917), founder of the Afro-American Realty Company. Payton credits his attendance at a meeting in 1902 in Richmond, Virginia. The meeting was organized by Washington's National Negro Business League. Payton asserted that the meeting was his inspiration in the founding of his Harlem company that was so instrumental in the development of a black Harlem.

By the 1930s, a disillusioned W.E.B. DuBois was advocating a black economic development program that was similar to Mr. Washington's 1900s Tuskegee-based program. Here are the words of DuBois, less than forty years after Washington's 1895 Atlanta Compromise Speech, writing in his 1940 autobiography *Dusk of Dawn*:

> *"We must organize our strengths as consumers; learn to cooperate and use machines and power as producers; train ourselves in methods of democratic control within our own group. Run and support our own institutions."*

Tuskegee-Trained Architect-Exports, 1902–1922

In 1902, John Lankford, the first Tuskegee-trained architect to arrive in Washington, DC, proceeded to establish a busy professional practice in the U Street corridor that was the physical heart of black Washington. Lankford became a vital business and economic-development entity immediately upon his arrival. Rigidly segregated Washington, DC, and its white architectural community's quest to develop the city as a world-class one, had no role or room for the likes of a John Lankford.

Apart from his immediate task of designing the True Reformers Building on U Street, NW, which is still standing today, Lankford went on to establish a local branch of Booker T. Washington's National Negro Business League. Lankford most probably saw the NBL as an appropriate counterpart to the American Institute of Architects (AIA), which he had no hope of joining. The True Reformers Building was constructed by a black general contractor with financing from the Washington, DC, black community.

Booker T. Washington considered Lankford one of his finest Tuskegee alumni. Much of Lankford's writing and speaking was in the Black Nationalist and Afrocentric mode. Mr. Washington was substantially in agreement with Lankford but could not be caught publicly uttering such views, which actually predated the great Marcus Garvey's black nationalist preaching by fifteen years. In a major speech, "The Negro as Architect and Builder," that Lankford delivered in New York City during that time, we can glimpse the worldview of this Tuskegee-trained architect. His nearly 100-year-old words represent contemporary

2.21 John Lankford. Source: Wikipedia Commons

2.22. True Reformers Building, 12th and U Streets, Washington, DC, completed 1903, restored 2012. Source: Author.

imperatives for the twenty-first century African American architect:

> Historians have recorded enough facts to give the world sufficient reason to believe that the black man, the Negro, in his native country among his own people, with his own black hands, over one thousand years before the Christian era, laid the foundations and erected some of the greatest monuments, buildings, and cities that have ever been designed or built by man.

Lest we think that Lankford's explicit allusions to himself as a builder was without literal significance—as was often the case when white architects sometimes rhetorically referred to themselves as builders—Lankford set the record straight. He articulated the structure of his multi-faceted office operations. He also made it clear that he viewed himself and others like him as frontline business leaders in their respective communities. We need hardly stretch our imaginations to grasp the scope of a contemporary black equivalent of Lankford's 1903 "finance-acquire-develop-design-build-manage" machine. His business card described him thusly:

> Expert builder, examiner and instructor. Plans gotten on short notice from rough sketches, pencil drawings and mailed to any section of the country. We make a specialty of church and hall designs and for *arranging loans* (author's italics)

The second Tuskegee architect to arrive in DC was William Sidney Pittman. Architect-scholar Richard Dozier places Pittman among the initial 1895 diploma class of graduating architects taught by Taylor at Tuskegee. Pittman went on to Drexel in Philadelphia and completed the undergraduate architecture program there.

Pittman returned to Tuskegee to teach before leaving to join Lankford in Washington in 1905. He left Lankford's office after a year to pursue his own practice. In 1907 Pittman married Portia Washington, Booker T. Washington's daughter. Pittman won a limited government-sponsored competition to design the Negro Building for the 1907 Jamestown Tercentennial fair in Virginia.

Around that time, a black fourteen-year-old Los Angeles newspaper boy saw the nationally circulated *Pittsburg Courier* newspaper that featured a story about the project and its Negro architect. In later years, that paperboy—Paul Revere Williams—wrote an article in which he alluded to the impact that newspaper article had on his aspirations for a career in architecture. Williams went on to be recognized as one of America's greatest architects.

Pittman went on to design another signature building for the black Washington community. Philanthropists Julius Rosenwald, John D. Rockefeller, and the YMCA each donated challenge funds to build a new structure on 12th Street just a short walk from Lankford's True Reformers Building on U Street. The YMCA was constructed by a black-owned construction firm based in Richmond, Virginia.

Architect Vertner Tandy (1885-1949) came to the New York scene in 1907 after receiving his architecture degree from Cornell. Before that Tandy had completed a certificate program in architectural drawing and building construction from

2.23 William Pittman.
Source: Wikipedia Commons

2.24 Portia Washington.
Source: Wikipedia Commons

2.25 Paul R. Williams
as a teenager.
Source: Wikipedia Commons

2.26. The Negro Building, Jamestown Tercentennial, 1907. Source: Wikipedia Commons

the Tuskegee program and under Robert Taylor's tutelage. In 1909, Tandy became the first black licensed architect in New York state. He designed numerous structures in Harlem that are still standing today.

Madam C.J. Walker (1867-1919), a millionaire hair-care tycoon and ardent follower of Booker T. Washington and his Negro Business League, entered into a long and mutually beneficial business relationship with Tandy. In addition to Villa Lewaro, her upstate New York mansion, Walker hired Tandy to design her brownstone townhouse and salon in Harlem. Both homes would become the retreats and gathering spots for many noted Harlem Renaissance activists.

2.27 12th Street YMCA, Washington, DC. Source: Wikipedia Commons

2.28 Vertner Tandy

2.29 Madam C.J. Walker.
Source: Wikipedia Commons

2.30 and 2.31. Front and rear view of Villa Lewaro the home of Madam C.J. Walker, Irvington, NY.
Source: Wikipedia Commons, Photo by David Bohl

3. The Harlem Renaissance: Missed Connections, 1919–1929

"American Negro history is basically a history of the conflict between integrationist forces and nationalist forces in politics, economics and culture, no matter what leaders are involved and what slogans are used."

—Harold Cruse, ca. 1967

3.1 Book Cover. Source: Author

Architect-author Norman Brosterman's compelling book, *Inventing Kindergarten* convincingly supports his contention about the impact of German kindergarten founder Friedrich Froebal's (1782-1852) educational philosophy on early twentieth century artists and architects. Brosterman shows how Froebal's philosophy influenced the course of Western art history over the last 150 years. Towering twentieth century figures ranging from Picasso to Frank Lloyd Wright had been trained in some variation of a Froebal kindergarten.

Brosterman asserted that "in effect the early Froebal-inspired kindergarten instructors created an enormous international program designed specifically to alter the mental habits of the general populace . . . nineteenth century children from Austria to Australia learned a new visual language. . . *kindergarten taught abstraction. . .. The triumph of Cubism and geometric abstraction came just as architects were searching for new modes of expression*" (author's italics).

The world's most famous and arguably gifted twentieth century architect's mother was a deep believer in Froebal's educational philosophy. She acquired the Froebal teaching tools, known simply as the Froebal gifts, and gave them to Frank Lloyd Wright when he was still a small child during the early 1870s. In the first decade of the twentieth century, Wright designed and built a series of modernist homes in suburban Chicago that are known universally as the *Prairie Houses*. The Robie House, completed in 1908 in the Oak Park suburb of Chicago, is considered the crown jewel of Wright's Prairie Houses. Wright's connection to the Froebal gifts is undeniable to anyone who has seen the gifts and is familiar with Wright's turn of the twentieth century decade Prairie Houses and civic buildings.

In 1910, Wright's published works began circulating in Europe, where they were intellectually and artistically devoured by the European architectural avant-garde.

3.2 The Robie House, Oak Park, Ill. Built ca 1910. Frank Lloyd Wright, architect.
Source: Wikipedia Commons

Some Europeans were also grappling—though unknowingly—with how to turn Pablo Picasso's West African mask and sculpture-derived Cubist paintings into architectural expressions.

3.3 Alain Locke.
Source: Moorland-Spingarn Research Center, Howard University Archives.

Enter Alain Locke, who had joined the Howard University faculty in 1912 after a series of distinguished academic achievements, including a Rhodes Scholarship. Before joining Howard, he stopped at Tuskegee, where he seriously considered an offer from Booker T. Washington.

By 1917, Locke was on the Howard campus, vigorously championing the cause of a "school of Negro art." By then, he was a major figure in the percolating Harlem Renaissance in New York, and on the Howard University campus in DC. Locke was urging the fine arts faculty and students to use their art to express the black experience and aesthetic:

Indeed, there are many attested influences of African art in French and German modernist art . . . the constructive lessons of African art are

among the soundest, and most needed art creeds today. . ..
Surely the liberating example of such art will be as marked an influence in the contemporary work of Negro artists as it has been
on leading modernists; Picasso, Modigliani, Matisse and others
too numerous to mention.

Alain Locke, 1925

However, Locke's influence on the still fledgling Howard architecture department during that torrid 1920–1930 Harlem Renaissance period is only tangen-
tially evident. Credible scholars acknowledge the derivative relationship of
turn-of-the-twentieth-century architecture to the Cubist art movement led by
Pablo Picasso and Georges Braque. This all ties into the grand icon of modern
architecture, Charles Edouard Jeanerette, or *Le Corbusier*, as he is universally
known. This seminal twentieth century architect was a painter who was captivated by Picasso's Cubist approach to art. That Cubist fascination quickly became
the defining characteristic of his architecture.

Locke was in contact with all of the influential black art figures based in New York.
Locke was an admirer of Aaron Douglas (1899-1979), who was producing Cub-
ist-inspired art work in the 1920s. Locke considered Douglas to be the leader of
the small group of black visual arts modernists. Locke chose Douglas to illustrate
his book *The New Negro* that heralded the 1920-1930 Harlem Renaissance years.

During the Howard architecture program years between 1920 and 1935, there
were essentially two American architectures. There was the near universally adopted architecture of the classic Greco-Roman world of 1500 that was showcased at Daniel Burnham's 1893 Chicago World's Fair.

The other architecture was an integral part of a social, cultural, and ideologi-
cal movement that was rampant throughout 1920s Western Europe. The new
avant-garde European-imported architecture, as well as Wright's quintessential
American Prairie Houses, was viewed by dominant conservative American elites
as highly suspect. Those same conservative elites placed Negro jazz and modern
architecture in the category of only being of interest
to the lowest classes and racial castes, as well as the
"amoral and socialistic cultural avant-garde." Art critic Robert Hughes, in his epic 1998 book *American
Visions,* places such attitudes in perspective for us:

> Attached to the idea that modern art was
> foreign was the notion that it was influ-
> enced by blacks and thus uncivilized...
> related to "a world full of jazz . . . sexual,
> convulsive, primitive."

Black culture and modern architecture failed to con-
nect in the 1920s during the Harlem Renaissance for
reasons that are varied and often complex. At the
time of the Harlem Renaissance, a young German
aristocrat and architect, Walter Gropius, was setting

3.4 Aaron Douglas.
Source: Wikipedia Commons

up the Bauhaus in Dessau, Germany. Gropius attracted a collection of architects and artists who advanced modernist architecture throughout Europe. The Europeans pursued architecture in conjunction with painting and sculpture. Some of them came to America and assumed posts in elite design schools. Modernism and its relationship to community development and social   housing was a raging issue among this growing avant-garde movement.

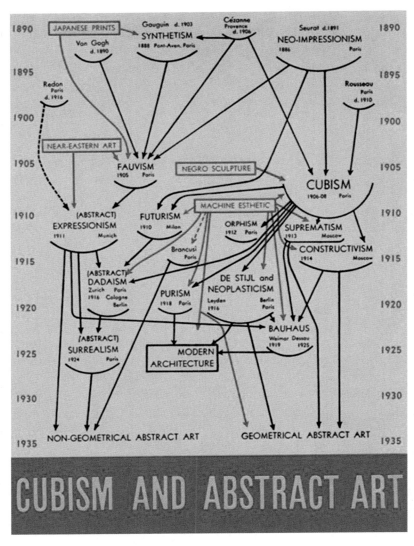

3.5. Alfred Barr Museum of Modern Art, 1936 diagram of the twentieth-century modern art and architecture movement. The "Negro Sculpture" at the center of this diagram contains the West African masks, sculpture, and art work discovered by Picasso in 1907 in a Paris museum. Picasso's discovery led him to Cubist art, which revolutionized Western art and architecture aesthetics. Source: Wikipedia Commons

We are also indebted to Harold Cruse for placing the Harlem Renaissance within a larger American context of time and cultural development. Cruse believed that the 1920s Renaissance was actually a culminating phase of a previous renaissance that started in 1910 with the initial growth of black Harlem. Before Cruse, Alain Locke was making pointed observations about the scope and depth of the Harlem Renaissance. I take the liberty to speculate that Locke thought architecture should have been a factor.

3.6. Les demoiselles d'Avignon, 1907 Picasso art work reputed to have been heavily influenced by his discovery of African masks. Source: Wikipedia Commons

The relationship between African art and Western modernism was at the very heart of the concerns of Locke and other theoreticians and activists of the Harlem Renaissance. In the early 1920s, Hilyard Robinson, a young Washington, DC native, was commuting to the University of Pennsylvania in Philadelphia to study in a Beaux-Arts program. He was spending summers in New York working for Vertner Tandy, a Robert Taylor-Tuskegee-trained and Cornell-trained architect who became the first black registered architect in New York in 1909. Robinson eventually became the head of Howard University's then still fledgling architecture program.

During that critical 1920–1930 decade of the Harlem Renaissance, Robinson and Tandy, like most other African American architects, had not yet strayed from their Beaux-Arts architecture indoctrination. Yet the notion that architecture was a critical cultural art form was *precisely* the position of the proselytizing European modernist architect. The white intellectuals who frequented Harlem and befriended black writers, poets, and artists during that time were of no help to the development of a black modernist architecture movement. At the turn of the twentieth century, the act of a white person listening to music in a club, buying recordings, viewing paintings in a gallery, or buying paintings by black people was not dependent on the establishment of personal relationships between equals.

Concurrent with the unfolding 1920s Harlem Renaissance movement in New York City, Los Angeles architect Paul Williams saw little prospect of building a practice that would primarily depend on the black community. Williams saw opportunity with a small elite group of wealthy white people with liberal to progressive-radical political leanings. Some elites found personal glorification in having a "Negro architect" design their home in eclectic, pre-modernist aesthetic styles.

Since the Harlem Renaissance, black music, black literature, and critical components of black visual and performing arts have been acclaimed the world over. So also, are the black men and women who have produced those art forms. The still new American nation's musical, artistic, and architectural expressions cannot be neatly categorized or compartmentalized from each other. There is consensus that the 250-year slavery experience of African Americans lay at the root of America's blues and jazz music. Inevitably, the same thing may have to be said about the new turn-of-the-twentieth-century modern art and architectural design aesthetic.

Hilyard Robinson would shortly become fully enmeshed in the modern architecture movement through his European travels after graduating from Columbia University, which was still Beaux-Arts dominated at the time. Robinson's nearest black counterparts on the New York City scene were architects such as John Lewis Wilson and Robinson's former summer employer, Vertner Tandy. Between 1923 and 1928, Wilson was also completing the Beaux-Arts curriculum at Columbia. By the early 1930s, agitation for new publicly funded housing development by Harlem community activists led to several large new housing projects, one that included Wilson as a member of a design team collaborative.

Wilson became one of the seven architects hired by the New Deal Works Projects Administration—the WPA. The charge of this architectural consortium was to design the sprawling six-hundred-unit Harlem River Houses Public Housing complex. The project opened for occupancy in 1937. During the Harlem Renaissance period, Wilson most likely held progressive social views about the emerging modern architecture movement and social housing but may not have felt that he was able to put those views into action on smaller projects under his control.

Lois Mailou Jones, a gifted black artist on the Howard campus by 1930, was a prime example of Locke's exhortation to black artists. Jones, in a small way, was eventually responsible for bridging the fine arts department and the architecture department through a course in watercolor painting that she taught every spring. Renowned black artist James Wells also offered a course in freehand drawing that was a freshman architecture course requirement.

Culturally, in the end, black architects were not able to heed the words of Duke Ellington, arguably the greatest cultural artist of twentieth century America. Ellington never lost sight of the fact that he was, in his own words, "writing Negro music." All the while, the true culture of Black America continues to create jazz, blues, and hip-hop music, cutting-edge film, dance, theater, and literature on a consistently world-class plane of excellence.

4. Howard University: "A Gentleman's Profession," 1919–1951

The evolution of architecture education at Howard University in Washington, DC, is best understood when placed in a larger context. By 1900, there were eleven American architecture schools, all patterned after the Paris École and its American model at MIT. While the Tuskegee-based architecture program (along with several other programs at industrial-oriented black colleges) was preparing students for a role of *master builder*, the white schools were intent on separating the role of architect from that of builder to the maximum extent possible.

This was the path laid out in architectural education for the American architect and how he would best function in the building of the dynamic, new American industrial landscapes. On the basis of American social structure and strivings, the bifurcation of the old master builder and the gentleman architect made sense. This was consistent with an upper-class image of high culture, refined taste, and irreproachable ethics. The gentlemanly architect was socialized to view himself as above the lowly world of construction rowdies and ruffians.

This view of how the world of building should work was logical at the time for a white world. That world had a parallel universe of builders, developers, financiers, suppliers, manufacturers, and craftsmen who could "make" things with their hands. This white parallel universe also had an abundance of wealthy capitalist–industrialist patrons and clients, and, most important, a political system.

4.1 Emmett Scott and Booker T. Washington.
Source: Moorland Spingarn Research Center, Howard University Archives, Howard University, Washington, DC.

Booker T. Washington died in 1915. His private secretary, Emmett J. Scott (1873-1957), left Tuskegee after Washington's death. Scott took a prominent position in the federal government in Washington, DC. While there, Scott was also affili-

4.2 William Augustus "Pops" Hazel. Source: Spingarn Research Center, Howard University Archives, Howard University, Washington, DC.

4.3 Albert I. Cassell. Source: Spingarn Research Center, Howard University Archives, Howard University, Washington, DC.

ated with Howard University. He may have been an influence in the Washington, DC, careers of several other Tuskegee transplants to the area.

By 1919, the center of architectural preparation had shifted from the Tuskegee campus to Howard University. Howard was developing the dominant black university-based program producing licensed African American architects.

In the 1940s, Hampton University in Virginia and Southern University in Louisiana also started architecture programs. However, US Census records over the 1920–1940 years never showed more than twenty black persons listed as licensed architects.

The Howard University architecture program was formally started in 1919 by former Tuskegee instructor William Augustus "Pops" Hazel (1854-1929). The vocational taint on the program and the DuBoisian vision of classical education permeating Howard made tensions inevitable. The old paradigm used in the building of the Tuskegee campus was not replicable at Howard. There was also the intuitive inclination of new incoming Ivy League-trained Howard faculty members to conform to the culture of the robust white architecture establishment situated just beyond the Howard campus.

A major preoccupation of the white architecture establishment was "professionalism." Essentially, this required establishing strict formal and ethical distinctions between the genteel (and increasingly university educated) architect and the builder.

There were several instances of attempts to replicate the Tuskegee modus operandi. Albert I. Cassell (1895-1969) landed at Howard shortly after the arrival of Hazel. Objective conditions and the spirit of the times may well have made resistance to following the same path that the white architects were pursuing difficult. Simply put, the doctrine of "professionalism" in architectural education at Howard from the 1920s onward was far more compatible with Howard's Du-Boisian classicist self-image.

The Booker T. Washington affiliated vocational pedagogy initially imported from Tuskegee was clearly suspect. Land ownership and development, training of construction and building mechanics, spun-off community businesses, and other critical aspects of black common culture characterized the Tuskegee model. Those issues were of less interest to Howard's incoming East Coast–trained African American architect–professors.

Cornell-educated Cassell had earlier partnered with Hazel in building on the Tuskegee campus and was solidly in line with the Booker T. Washington-inspired nationalist ideology and modus operandi. Cassell succeeded Hazel as the leader of the department in 1920. Cassell occupied that position until the arrival in 1926 of Mordecai Johnson, Howard's first black president.

Johnson immediately appointed Cassell as Campus Architect in charge of producing all master plans for the development of the campus. The assignment also included the actual design of major buildings that would eventually include the iconic Founders Library and Frederick Douglass Hall. Cassell collaborated with Cornell-trained black landscape architect David Williston, who also had been the chief landscape architect at Tuskegee in 1910.

As department chair, Cassell hired young DC-born architect Hilyard R. Robinson (1899-1986) to teach part-time in 1924. Cassell passed the department chair on to Robinson two years later. In 1929 Robinson relinquished the chair position to young Howard Hamilton Mackey (1901-1987), a University of Pennsylvania graduate.

Robinson was on a mission to complete his master's degree work at Columbia in 1931. After doing so, Robinson went on a nearly year-long tour of Europe with an intense study of European modernist architects and their best social-housing projects before returning to DC.

In 1931, Mackey organized an exhibition of the work of the handful of African American architects practicing around the country. Mackey's pivotal Howard University Art Gallery exhibit included the work of Robert Taylor of Tuskegee, Paul Williams of Los Angeles, Calvin McKissack of Nashville, Tennessee, and other practitioners based in Chicago and Honolulu. The work of Mackey, Robinson, and Cassell was also showcased. The exhibit received coverage in the Washington Post that lead to further coverage in several national mainstream outlets as well as the national black press outlets.

Robinson was strongly identifying with the Congress Internationale Architects Moderne—better known as CIAM. His becoming a card-carrying member was improbable, but he did have access. This association of socially progressive European architects and planners began meeting regularly in 1928. On his return

4.4 Hilyard R. Robinson.
Sources: Moorland-Spingarn Research
Center, Manuscript Division Howard
University, Washington DC

4.5 Howard Hamilton Mackey.
Sources: Moorland-Spingarn Research
Center, Manuscript Division Howard
University, Washington DC

from Europe in 1931, Robinson rejoined the Howard architecture faculty. Robinson was by then also strongly identifying with the Harlem Renaissance "New Negro" idea. Robinson stressed that black architects had to address the pioneering work required by the social realities of the black masses. In his papers in the Spingarn-Moreland collection at Howard, I found the following direct quote by Robinson:

> Our teaching must reflect the fact that the young Negro trained as an architect, handling problems originating essentially among the Negro masses, urban and rural, still has the work of a pioneer to do.

Robinson's words echo Booker T. Washington's concern for practical solutions to the dire plight of the Negro masses but also captured the spirit of DuBois by providing uplifting leadership for the masses via a classics-educated talented tenth. This is a tension in architectural education at black universities that still awaits resolution to this day.

Robinson most certainly already knew Los Angeles–based Paul Williams, but Mackey's 1931 exhibit may have been a major contributing factor that led to the fruitful bi-coastal partnership the two men formed. By 1934, Robinson had completed the groundwork in acquiring a contract to design the 274-unit Langston Terrace Public Housing Project. Robinson demonstrated great entrepreneurial skill and political acumen in acquiring this career-establishing design commission.

With his still small practice at the core, Robinson structured a "salt and pepper" architectural team. He joined with Williams, who by the early 1930s had built an impressive commercial and residential practice in Los Angeles. Robinson also pulled in a respected and politically connected local white architect, Irving Porter. This shrewd relationship with Williams would lead to Robinson's receiving Howard University commissions that would have been politically difficult for the university to justify otherwise. Federal overseers still retained control of critical aspects of campus development.

Williams, just five years older than Robinson, was born in Los Angeles in 1884. By the time he was twenty-one years old in 1905, Williams had attained a state of California contractor's license. In 1921 Williams acquired his California architect license. Later, Williams recalled in his memoirs advice that he received from one of his high school teachers after confiding his intent to become an architect: Williams can be paraphrased as having said that he was told that "no white client would engage a black person in such a capacity, and that his own people don't have any use for architects."

Williams shared much in common with DC-based Robinson. Williams was a modernist who also designed in the Beaux-Arts, Georgian, and Federalist styles. Robinson felt that Williams' robustly romanticist approach to architecture was a perfect match for his own virtually exclusive commitment to the avant-garde international-style modernism that is expressed in his Langston Terrace project.

4.6. Hilyard Robinson and Paul Williams in Williams' DC office ca 1938.
Source: Spingarn Research Center, Howard University Archives, Howard University, Washington, DC

While Williams was devoted to the idea of the working-class modern house (he published several books on the subject), Robinson was devoted to the idea of modern housing as social reform for the Negro masses.

Robinson had completely reinvented himself since his undergraduate days at Columbia in the 1920s. Along the way, he received strategic help from white progressive-minded (usually Jewish) government officials. He became one of the nation's foremost black public housing design authorities. His Langston Terrace project, completed in 1938 in partnership with Williams, won positive reviews from widely respected architecture critics. The project was exhibited at the Museum of Modern Art in New York City. Renowned critic and planner–sociologist Lewis Mumford acclaimed Langston Terrace as being equal to the finest modernist social housing being constructed throughout Europe at that time.

From 1947 to 1967, Hilyard Robinson ran a very influential "teaching office" within walking distance of the Howard campus. Robinson's office played a major role in launching the offices of several other black Washington, DC firms. Several of the men in those firms went on to play similar roles of incubating black-owned architectural firms in Washington, DC and beyond.

The utilization of African American architects to design buildings on the Howard campus continued but with a different and more orthodox business arrangement than the one utilized initially between Albert Cassell and Howard. University commissions began to go increasingly to the recently established off-campus offices of the joint-venturing practices of Robinson in DC and Williams of Los Angeles

At that same time, Robinson was starting to mingle with the emerging European masters he had met earlier in Europe and who were now in America. By 1937, around the time that Frank Lloyd Wright was completing Bear Run, which was universally regarded as a masterpiece of the twentieth century, Robinson was witnessing the opening of *his* masterpiece, Langston Terrace, in DC. Robinson's Langston Terrace, along with Wright's Fallingwater House at Bear Run were featured in April 4, 2016 in a Public Broadcast Corporation televised documentary billed as the ten most important houses in America in the twentieth century.

In 1941, Robinson sought out and received a major U.S. War Department commission to design an air base at Tuskegee, Alabama. This required his joining forces with McKissack and McKissack, a family firm in Nashville, Tennessee. The McKissack firm, established in 1905, was the first black-owned architectural firm in Tennessee. The Tuskegee air base was to be used to train the nation's first black combat pilots for World War II, much to the consternation of powerful white politicians, War Department civilians, and military officers. Those people were deeply vested in the white supremacy-based belief that the term *black combat pilot* was an impossibility.

The site chosen by the War Department for the proposed airfield was topographically and hydrologically challenged. An incorrectly designed grading and drainage plan would have resulted in disasters that would have doomed the entire Tuskegee Airmen project. Robinson's travels throughout the European low

4.7 Langston Terrace Dwellings, Benning Road, NE Washington, DC

4.8. Langston Terrace Dwellings, Courtyard.
Sources: Spingarn Research Center, Howard University Archives, Howard University, Washington, DC

countries during World Wars I as a military officer and World War II as a visiting architect gave him a familiarity with drainage design that came in handy on this project.

The McKissack firm, then headed by brothers Moses and Calvin, was certified as architects, engineers, and general building contractors, a first in a Deep South state. For this project, the War Department accepted the proposition of Robinson serving as design and production architect–engineer of record with the McKissacks as the general contractors who would build the $6.1 million project ($100 million in today's dollars).

By 1938, Albert Cassell and Howard University parted company. Like Robinson, Cassell went on to develop a successful Washington, DC, private practice. His most notable and enduring built work was the four hundred–unit Mayfair Mansions apartments in far northeast DC for middle-class black citizens. The project's construction began in 1942. Cassell designed, developed, and

4.9 Tuskegee fighter pilots, ca 1945. Source: Wikipedia Commons

4.10. Tuskegee Army Airfield, Tuskegee 99th Pursuit Squad, completed in 1941, Hilyard R. Robinson, architect, McKissack & McKissack, general contractors. Source: Wikipedia Commons

oversaw the construction. This was a follow-on variation of Robinson's Langston Terrace project of federally assisted housing for black citizens aspiring to the middle class.

Mackey, Cassell, and Robinson all benefitted greatly from the presence of progressive-minded white public officials in the local DC government and the federal national housing agency. These officials pushed to include African American architects on the design teams of large wartime-era public housing projects for blacks in Washington, DC.

Clearly, Cassell, Robinson, and Mackey were all passionately committed to providing housing to the "Negro masses" in Washington, DC, and across the nation. But they also had an architecture program at Howard that had to receive formal national accreditation. The effectiveness of the three Howard professors in passing on the urgency of their commitment to initiating and designing large housing projects for black Washingtonians to the next generation of Howard-trained African American architects is not in dispute. However, clearly the succeeding generations of architects were not able to overcome other race-based socio-economic forces that ultimately lead to the decline of public housing in DC.

These three architects wrote or published sparingly beyond the narrowest technical level. In retrospect, we know how vitally important an architect's lengthy writing and proselytizing on design theories and philosophies has been in establishing reputations. These architects were also without the benefit of architectural historians or influential patrons championing their cause.

The Howard faculty felt compelled to seek the imprimatur of the still rigidly segregated and racist-minded white architectural professional and educational establishment. Over the period from 1926 to 1951 the goal of attaining national accreditation was the top priority of every faculty member and administrator at Howard. This would be the first black university-based program in the nation to achieve the distinction of full national accreditation. Mackey, Robinson, and Louis E. Fry, Sr. were all compelled to prepare people who would more resemble the white world's version of the evolving genteel architect. The architectural

4.11. Mayfair Mansions apartments, Northeast Washington, DC. Source: Wikipedia Commons

education philosophy and professional practice modus operandi of the three Howard educators was the same *professionalism* that the larger white architectural establishment was pursuing.

After becoming accredited in 1951, Howard went on to graduate scores of architects, including a few who were not African Americans and several who could be classified as white. These graduates returned to various parts of the United States, the Caribbean Isles, Haiti, Puerto Rico, the West African nations of Liberia, Ghana, Nigeria, several other Eastern and Middle Eastern countries, India, Iran, and Israel.

Looking back, we can see three distinctive variations of professional practice agendas for African American architects by the early to middle twentieth century. There was the 1882-1920s Taylor–Tuskegee branch of architecture as black social and economic development, the nationalist model. There was the 1930-1960s Hilyard Robinson-Howard University branch of elite professionals engaging in genteel advocacy for black socio-economic uplift. There was also the Paul Williams branch, which was a "vindication of the race" variation of the 1930-68 Robinson-Howard branch. The common thread of the three variations continue to this day to be anchored in orthodox professional practice. This is the continuing reality despite an offshoot of Black Power movement activism by Howard University architects from 1968 era up to the present.

PART II

ARCHITECTS AND BLACK AMERICA 1951–2019

"BLACK POWER,
BLACK MAYORS,
BLACK ARCHITECTS"

---

5. An Early First Draft Personal Memoir, 1944–1972

Preteen to Licensed Architect

Despite having recently acquired official membership in the octogenarian wing of the senior citizen's club, my memories are still vivid about being dragged away, kicking and screaming, in the dead of night at age seven in 1946. Shortly after my seventh birthday my mother returned to New Orleans and announced to all within earshot that night that she was taking me to live in California. I was then enjoying idyllic childhood days in New Orleans. My life was suddenly interrupted by my beautiful and distant young mother, who had left Louisiana to resettle in Los Angeles when I was an infant.

I was also spending wondrous, lazy summers in the "country" as we called it back then. Those summers were being spent living in the house of my mother's mother, Mama Maude in Bayou Goula, a little rural sugar cane plantation village just outside Baton Rouge. I spent the rest of the year living the life of a pampered little prince in the home of my father's mother, Mama Mary, in the Gert Town section of New Orleans .

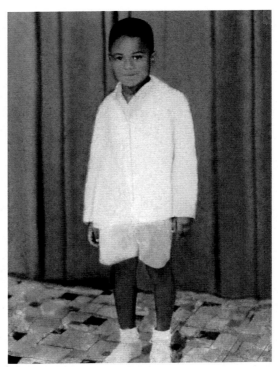

5.1 Author, age 5 in 1944, New Orleans.
Source: Author

Mama Mary's house was a short walk from the campus of historically black Xavier University. I had been born in the New Orleans Charity Hospital just a few blocks beyond the French Quarter. My smart, high-spirited, tart-tongued, "Louisiana red-bone" mother was about eighteen years old and still single. Her name was Viola Derizan, and her biological father was a black Creole who lived in New Roads City in Pointe Coupee Parish, where my mother was born. Point Coupee is about twenty miles north of Baton Rouge. I had never met "Papa" but was raised on many tall tales about him. I especially remember one about how he got my then fifteen-year-old grandma Mama Maude pregnant but refused to marry her or fully embrace ownership of my mother.

While my mother was pregnant with me in 1939, my father left town and joined the Civilian Conservation Corps. He eventually ended up in France as a U.S. army soldier in World War II. Eight years after my conception, the two of them would somehow rendezvous nearly 1,700 miles away from New Orleans in South Central Los Angeles. They ended up getting married there. After my mother came back to New Orleans to retrieve me (and a younger sister who had come along in my father's war time absence) I would lay eyes on him for the very first time on my arrival in Los Angeles shortly before my eighth birthday. He was an illiterate common laborer who was prone to bouts of drinking that sometimes unleashed a violently abusive side of his normally bland personality.

I grew up in the Jordan Downs public housing project in the Watts section of South-Central Los Angeles. The four of us—my father treated my sister as though she were his own flesh and blood—always had enough to eat at home. My own daily 5 a.m. *Los Angeles Times* paper route kept me in pocket money for movies, hamburgers, and 78 rpm "rhythm and blues" records (anything by Louis Jordan and his Tympani Five, or "doo-wop" singing groups). Just as important, we—along with much of the rest of the section of the "projects" where I lived—transported, practically intact, to Watts many of the food preferences and religious rituals of our richly textured black New Orleans culture .

At least three times each year there would be a steaming pot of "file' gumbo," filled with shrimp, crab, oysters, chicken, smoked sausage, and beef stew meat. There were also red kidney beans (with cut up smoked sausages when times were good) over white rice several times a week. Our little church services had some of the same mysterious Haitian "voodoo" overtones overlapping the fire and brimstone Baptist church jam sessions that I remembered from Louisiana.

By my early junior high school years, I had developed a serious reading habit, centered on novels like the terrifying and occasionally erotic *Dracula* classic by Bram Stoker. My reading habit was carefully hidden from some—but by no means all—of my housing project peers. The "projects" of sixty-five years ago were very different from those of the last quarter of the twentieth century. In *my* housing project, none of my friends ever got shot, there were no "drugs" to speak of, the occasional pregnancy of an unwed neighborhood girl usually resulted in a hasty "shotgun" wedding, and nearly everyone had a father at home.

I can recall no childhood dreams about wanting to "build things." There were no blinding-light epiphanies about becoming an architect. I indirectly drifted toward architecture through the simple matter of having to decide between two vocational tracks upon entering senior high school in 1954. I had to pick between "wood-shop" and "mechanical drafting." The drafting thing aligned squarely with my well-developed aversion to working at what I disdainfully viewed as manual labor in the shop courses.

The third choice of pursuing a college prep track, which could have led to enrollment at the University of Southern California or Cal–Berkeley, was simply not conceivable to me at that time and place in my life. My high school drafting teacher was a gentle and elderly white man whom I knew only as Mr. Welty. He always treated me as his most prized protégée. I was the first one of his students to capture one of the three cash prizes in a prestigious annual citywide mechanical drawing contest for Los Angeles high school students. All of my high school friends and teachers knew that in the Los Angeles of the 1950s, the mechanical drawing skills that I had become most known for could lead to a decent-paying job right out of high school.

Upon graduation in 1957, I did indeed land a job as an entry-level draftsman. During my first year out of high school and at my new downtown office job—ten miles away from my isolated Watts neighborhood in South Central Los Angeles—I overheard several of the architecture school graduates in the office raving about a juicy novel that was supposedly a fictionalized account of the early life

5.2 Author, age 17 in 1956 in Los Angeles.
Source: Author

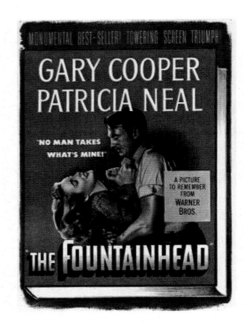

5.3. Book Cover. Source: Author

of Frank Lloyd Wright, the great architect. I found the book *The Fountainhead* by Ayn Rand. The book became a movie with Rand's anti-hero architect Howard Roark played by Gary Cooper.

I could not put the book down until I had finished it. However, the possibility of actually becoming a licensed, practicing architect still had not occurred to me.

After graduating from high school, I still lived in the projects in Watts. I had become a minor celebrity of sorts because of landing a job as a local government draftsman with permanent civil-service status. In the eyes of all of my peers, I was set for life. I had actually exceeded the hopes of my parents as well as some—but by no means all—of my teachers.

During my first year out of high school I was right at the cusp of matrimony with my senior high school-year sweetheart—a stunningly pretty, almond-eyed girl with a deep ebony complexion. She still haunts my memories to this day. We were both convinced that my Los Angeles County draftsman job was paying me enough money to support a family. I was as madly in love as eighteen-year-olds are capable of. But the growing notion of becoming an architect was starting to overpower the essentially passion-driven need to get married. I became consumed by my struggle to prepare myself for admission to a reputable university architecture school. I had accumulated mostly mechanical drawing courses on my high school transcript, and I had not saved very much money. While I did manage to earn a varsity letter in a tough inner-city high school football league, I was not even remotely in the zone of consideration for an athletic scholarship to a reputable university.

During my second year of working downtown and going to night school at East Los Angeles Community College (we called it *junior college* back then), the November 1958 issue of *Ebony* magazine ran a splashy photo-feature article entitled "Successful Young Architects." That article—in conjunction with my having just finished reading Ayn Rand's *The Fountainhead*—was indeed that blinding-light epiphany.

I had no clue that Rand's book was just a right-wing political tract. But judging by the ages of many of my African American architect peers around the country today, I wasn't the only one affected by that electrifying *Ebony* article or Rand's galvanizing book. The *Ebony* article estimated the existence of just over a 100 licensed Negro architects around the country (out of an estimated national total of 20,000 licensed American architects). The article was also actually my first exposure to a small but growing contingent of black Los Angeles architects other than the already legendary Paul Williams.

I was even more enthralled by young New Yorker and Columbia University graduate Daniel Watts, who was prominently featured in the article. I began to entertain fantasies of immediately packing up and heading for New York with the hope of meeting Watts and getting his help in enrolling in Columbia's evening program. Instead, I started making regular visits to the University of Southern California campus in mid–South Central Los Angeles. On those visits, I would stroll through the architecture school and daydream. I dreamt mostly about how I was going to save the tuition money I needed to enroll at USC.

SUCCESSFUL YOUNG ARCHITECTS

5.4. Dan Watts, architect and Columbia University graduate, posing in front of New York's Idlewild airport terminal, which he had designed while employed by the Skidmore Owings and Merrill architectural firm. Source: Ebony Magazine, November 1958. Wikipedia Commons

After two years of working for the county government, I was able to land a junior draftsman job at a downtown private-sector architectural firm. The firm hired me on the basis of my drawings in an architectural drafting course I had completed at East Los Angeles City College. My instructor, a stern Egyptian-American architect whom I knew as Mr. Hasuna, had connections at USC and was determined to get me into the School of Architecture. After six months, I ventured farther west to Beverly Hills and worked at a smaller but very busy Jewish-owned architectural firm. That job lasted for another six months. However, three years after high school graduation, I still had not accumulated enough money to play the "Joe College" full-time architecture-student role I longed for. The solution to my dilemma came in the form of a flyer from the U.S. Army recruitment office. I could volunteer to be drafted immediately at age twenty-one.

Before leaving Los Angeles to head north to the Bay Area to start army duty in 1960, I became aware that Paul Williams was the architect for the Golden State

5.5. Golden State Mutual Headquarters Building, Los Angeles ca 1959.
Source: Author.

Mutual Insurance Company headquarters building, which was right around the corner from where I then lived. This was the iconic building that symbolized the black businesses in Los Angeles. I never tired of passing this building and entering the sleek modernist lobby every chance I got.

I was inducted into the army in the late winter of 1960. After completing basic training at Fort Ord, California (and spending glorious weekends in nearby Monterey, and several Saturday nights at the Black Hawk Jazz Club in San Francisco), the army sent me to the Fort Belvoir Army Engineering Center right outside of Washington, DC. In DC there were more glorious weekend nights spent in the 14th and U Streets area darting back and forth between the old Bohemian Caverns nightclub, Abart's Lounge, and the Hollywood Nightclub. I once actually caught Miles Davis *and* John Coltrane in the same week. I also caught the act of an unknown young comedian named Bill Cosby during that time.

Near the end of my two years on active army duty, I applied to and was accepted at Howard University with advanced standing credits for my completed junior college courses in Los Angeles. I also had acceptance letters from the architecture schools at the University of Oregon in Eugene, and Cal Poly San Luis Obispo, about a three-hour drive north of Los Angeles. I also knew that the U.S. Army owed me a cash payout to cover my plane fare back to Los Angeles. There were no restrictions on how I had to use that money. As fate would have it, the amount was large enough to cover my first semester tuition installment payment at Howard University. This got me through to my first G.I. Bill check.

In the fall of 1962, at the ripe old age of twenty-three, I was all set to enroll as a first-year student—a freshman—in the fully accredited and apparently highly respected five-year Bachelor of Architecture program at Howard University. That degree was the first required hurdle I had to clear in order to become a licensed architect and eventually open my own office. I was clueless and entirely unaware of the social issues that would literally explode in Washington, DC, six years later. I was even more in the dark about the explosions that would take place back home in Los Angeles in the summer of 1965. One issue in particular that turned out to play a huge role in my eventual radicalization was a 550-acre neighborhood lying literally in the shadow of the national Capitol building.

This Southwest DC community of very poor and ill-housed people was undergoing urban renewal, or as most Black Americans saw matters, *Negro removal*. By

5.6 DC Southwest DC black community before urban renewal clearance.
Source: Wikipedia Commons

5.7. Southwest DC upscale development in 1965 after urban renewal clearance. Source: Wikipedia Commons

the time I graduated from Howard in 1967, that same neighborhood and parcel of land looked decidedly different from what it had a decade earlier. The social and economic turmoil of those relocated residents was a root cause of the turmoil that would explode across DC over the following decade.

When I first arrived at the Howard University School of Architecture, I thought I had died and gone to heaven. The 100,000 square feet, four story School of Engineering and Architecture Building that I was going to spend the next five years practically living in had been designed by my idol Paul R. Williams (I soon learned that it was designed by a joint venture team of Williams and Hilyard Robinson).

There, on Howard's campus, I was bumping into not just architects, but *African American* architects;

5.8 Downing Hall School of Engineering & Architecture. Source: Author

black licensed architects, with not only bachelor's degrees but also master's degrees from Ivy League schools! Never in my wildest imagination had I encountered anything like the Howard University campus. Howard's predominately black faculty of architects, engineers, PhDs, medical doctors, lawyers, scientists, and obviously very bright students was all a pleasant cultural shock.

During my freshman year, my already acquired oversized "architect's ego" affectation caused me to blow an opportunity for a job in the office of Hilyard Robinson, the great man himself. While working in Los Angeles in 1959, I had posed the question to a black co-worker of whether the great Paul Williams had a black counterpart of similar status elsewhere around the country. Only Robinson's name came up.

My hard-won interview with Robinson was an unfortunate hour of confrontational exchanges about what he viewed as my inflated views about my abilities. An exasperated Robinson abruptly ended the interview when I arrogantly informed him of my "non-negotiable" hourly rate expectations. That rate, unknown to me then, was higher than what he was paying Howard architecture school graduates.

Little did I realize at the time, that I would become part of a first wave of Howard graduates hired by downtown Connecticut Avenue white firms. Before I arrived, the established norm for Howard architecture graduates was to take jobs in the uptown Black DC Georgia Avenue offices of earlier Howard graduates. The other option was in the offices of a small group of Jewish architects.

Only forty years had passed between the 1923 arrival at Howard University of Howard Mackey from Philadelphia and my own arrival in September 1962 when Mackey was the department chair. The black Washington architectural world I entered in 1962 was one of optimism. Our faculty was quite confident in our ability to transcend the blatantly racist patterns dominating much of the local architecture profession. During those 1960s days, virtually all private commercial commissions and institutional work went to white firms. Most public-sector design contracts of substance and prestige coming out of city government were firmly earmarked for white firms. Looking back, and using today's vernacular, white Washington, DC, architects were the beneficiaries of the "mother of all 'affirmative action' and 'set-aside' programs."

Jewish architects were a key part of the teaching faculty. By the 1950s, those men served as the bridge between the separate worlds of Washington's white architects and the small but growing group of African American architects. On the day I arrived to begin my studies, the faculty contained six black and three white full-time professors.

In 1947, Leon Brown, a Jewish architect with a small, thriving Georgetown practice, was one of the first practitioners to integrate his office by hiring Howard graduates. Shortly after that, Dean Mackey strategically recruited Brown to the faculty. Brown was a very decent and amiable man with a racially liberal mindset. He became the department's ambassador to the white world of Washington architecture. Leon Brown was naturally given the nickname of *Vanilla Brown* as the counterpart to our other beloved black (and crypto-Garveyite) professor, Leroy John Henry Brown , who was affectionately known to upper-division architecture students as *Chocolate Brown*.

I distinctly remember Leon Brown's courses in architectural interiors and theory of architecture, as well as his tutelage as a design studio critic. While many Howard architecture students of that period were from black middle- and even upper-class backgrounds, their worlds were still separate from the needs, styles, tastes, and perceptions of white upper-class Washington. This group was our presumed ultimate clientele. Leon Brown managed to shed light on strange elite WASP customs for most of us. This was especially helpful for me, coming as I did from the public housing projects in Los Angeles.

5.9 Leroy "Chocolate" Brown, ca. 1965. Source: Courtesy of Dreck Wilson

The Black and Jewish faculty's commitment to heroic modern architecture was typical of new converts. They were uncompromising in their quest to ensure that the nearly all-black graduates of the program would be capable of earning a living wage in the white world of architecture. I enjoyed a special relationship with Leon Brown. He was the most cosmopolitan of the three original Jewish faculty members hired by Chairman Mackey.

Other practicing Jewish architects joined the faculty at Howard as adjuncts. Before I graduated in

1967, the most notable catch was Mort Hoppenfeld, who was a big deal for the program. Hoppenfeld had been hired earlier by the now legendary late James Rouse, founder of the new town of Columbia, Maryland, located between DC and Baltimore. Nearly all of the faculty members maintained small practices along with their teaching schedules at Howard.

I cannot recall having a serious discussion or lecture session with any of my Jewish instructors about the real business and economics of architecture as a real estate-based enterprise. However, I sincerely doubt that any of them other than Hoppenfeld actually knew anything about the subject or even cared about the subject.

There was indeed a main source of friction and disagreement that would inevitably develop between the 1960s Black Power wing of the architecture student body and our Jewish faculty (and several of our integrationist-minded African American faculty). Midway through my stay as a student we wanted to do and talk about things and issues in design studios and history classes that had been previously glossed over. On the even more fundamental issue of design contracts for high-profile, publicly financed projects in the black community, conflicts with Jewish firms were there, however well managed through civility and professional courtesies.

There were Jewish firms in DC that had established records of accomplishment and linkages within the still largely WASP-dominated old boy network of unelected officials controlling architect selections in government agencies. There is no question that the Black Power move- ment caused a number of major design con- tracts to be diverted to black firms. Several of these projects were ones that white as well as Jewish firms had every expectation of getting, as they had in the past.

Clearly, Jewish architects have been no dif- ferent from the larger Jewish community in their historic role of championing the cause of justice for African Americans. Therefore, I know how deeply and justifiably wounded many of my Jewish faculty friends and class- mates were at several sickening spectacles of anti-Semitism that inevitably cropped up during those turbulent times.

By the start of my fifth (and final) year in the fall of 1966, serious black consciousness was permeating the entire student body in the architecture school. This was all much to the acute discomfort of much of the facul- ty. We further rubbed faculty nerves raw by inviting Student Nonviolent Coordinating Committee (SNCC) big guns Stokely Carmi- chael and Courtland Cox to our jury reviews

5.10 Author and wife, Gerry, who was three months pregnant with son Mar- cus. June 1967.
Source: Author.

of controversial urban renewal projects. Carmichael and Cox were recent liberal arts graduates who welcomed our invitations as opportunities to engage our faculty in sometimes heated Black Power debates.

By the time I graduated in June of 1967 the movement was raging. Those were the turbulent late 1960s times of national unrest, war protests, civil rights turmoil, and urban street violence. We wanted very much to be relevant players in the movement. As an architecture graduates, that was a dubious proposition. The sixties' movements were about politics and above all culture and power, as in Black Power.

In New York City, in the heart of Harlem, there was an organization flying under the name, Architects Renewal Committee of Harlem, also simply known as ARCH. The ARCH founders and top leadership were socially conscious white Ivy League architecture professors and students. ARCH was a leading light in a mostly East Coast movement of several groups with similar motivations. These groups – calling themselves "advocate planners" - came to be known as being about "designing for the poor." They all appeared to have plenty of mainstream foundation support. Needless to say, none of this sat well with those of us in the Black Power movement.

High on rage and low on imagination, several of my classmates and I countered by calling ourselves Black Advocate Planners. Our problem with white advocate designers and planners was very much the same as SNCC's problem with some of the white radicals in the Southern civil rights campaign. We were enraged. These were our people, and we should be getting the resources and recognition to redesign our own communities.

Meanwhile, every culture-related academic discipline or department on Howard's campus was proudly adopting the black prefix. There was black art, black theater, black music, black literature, black film, black dance, and black social sciences—all integral parts of a universally acknowledged black culture. However, the Howard architecture faculty fiercely resisted any association or conflation of architecture with black(ness). We simply felt strongly that African American architects and planners should provide the leadership in redeveloping beleaguered black communities. Black residents, budding politicians, and sympathetic black bureaucrats invariably felt the same way. Serious-minded white radicals also shared our views about the importance of black leadership.

April 4, 1968

On the balmy spring evening of April 4, 1968, myself and three of my former Howard University architecture school classmates, by then a black nationalist architect-planners group known as 2MJQ , were sitting around in our office. The first letter in each of our last names were arranged to coincide with the famed Modern Jazz Quartet's popular name of MJQ. Our office was in the DC Shaw area community near Howard's campus. We were busy debating the tactics and grand strategies of the by then searing hot Black Power movement sweeping

5.11. 14th Street near U Street, NW Wash., DC, ca. April 5, 1968.
Source: Wikipedia Commons

America and DC. Suddenly, someone poked a head through our front door and yelled, "Turn on the radio . . . they've shot Martin Luther King!"

Barely a year out of Howard's architecture school, my initial gut reaction was about the same as many other very angry people throughout Black America. We all said in near unison: "This is it! . . . The Man is testing our resolve and fire-power! . . . It's time to haul out the guns." Some people did just that. I, on the other hand, and in typical armchair revolutionary fashion, remembered that I did not own a gun, and had not fired one since my 1960 army basic training days back at Fort Ord, California. So, I went home to my wife and three-month-old son, Marcus, who I named after the great 1920s Harlem based black nationalist icon, Marcus Garvey.

By the next day I was back at our community design center, which was also right around the corner from Stokely Carmichael's storefront headquarters. By then he was known also as Shaka Zulu as well as Kwame Touré. Our shops were near the corner of 14th and U Streets. We could observe the goings and comings of Carmichael and future DC Mayor Marion Barry, then also a SNCC heavyweight.

Both of them were dressed in the uniforms du jour; the big Afro hairdo and colorful African-print dashiki over a black knit turtleneck shirt was the uniform of choice for most of the college-educated militants. Barry and Carmichael were trying desperately to corral the raging fury of the angry crowd milling in the streets near the 14th and U Street intersection. By 6 a.m. the next morning the whole storefront block of 14th Street from U Street to W Street was in flames.

A major breakthrough exception to the growing trend of white advocate plan-ners in black urban areas was the reinvention of the formerly all-white advo-cacy planning group known as the Architects Renewal Committee of Harlem, commonly known as ARCH. By 1968, leadership of the foundation-funded ARCH was passed to Max Bond, a black Harvard-trained architect. Under Bond's leadership, aesthetic and formal concerns were immediately displaced in favor of more intensive efforts at initiating social action programs within Harlem. Bond was no ordinary architect.

During those incendiary Black Power–charged times, Bond brought the ultimate jaw-dropping credential into a highly skeptical Harlem community of rampant black nationalist sentiments. A few years after graduating from the Harvard Graduate School of Design in 1958, Bond took his considerable skills to Black Africa's first independent state , Ghana. Bond designed and built public facilities for Kwame Nkrumah's state design and construction arm. He also helped train young Ghanaians in the fledgling architecture school at the University of Science and Technology, Kumasi. Once we clearly grasped the full implications of Bond and the rejuvenated ARCH, my group, 2MJQ, was slipping up to Harlem to sit at the feet of Max Bond to observe, listen, and learn.

We managed to get the attention of the great white liberal icon Tom Wicker, erstwhile columnist of the *New York Times*. Our "black architects for black communities" rhetoric was highly offensive to conservative elements of the Black Intelligentsia. One highly respected Howard academic wrote a blistering condemnation of a flattering article Wicker wrote in the *New York Times* extolling our little movement. We proudly took that put-down rebuttal as a version of the NAACP's venerable Roy Wilkens' tirade against our new icon, Stokely Carmichael, and our new religion of Black Power. (Wilkins had earlier proclaimed that "Black Power is Black Death.")

5.12. 2MJQ Black Advocate Planners: Casey Mann, Melvin Mitchell, Robert Jayson, Harry Quintana, in our Shaw Urban Renewal Area Washington DC community design studio 1968. Source: Author

On our home turf in DC, the older established African American architects found us fascinating and useful. Some members of the old crowd were acting out of genuinely repressed black nationalist sentiments. Others were simply pragmatic opportunists who understood the business development implications of our militancy. We found it necessary to redefine our base and source of African American architectural and planning manpower to counteract the white threat to our own agenda of exclusively planning and designing for the Black Power movement. We identified any historically black university east of the Mississippi with an architecture or city-planning program as an "environmental planning" program.

From early April in 1968 to January 1969 my 2MJQ group of militant rabble-rousers and I were right in the middle of the feverish activities of recovery and rebuilding. By June of 1968, the turmoil of urban violence sweeping the nation was bringing about profound rethinking in many quarters. The Harvard Graduate School of Design (HGSD) responded by hiring a black professor of architecture. After a national search HGSD's choice was Jerome Lindsey, Howard architecture program's most heavily credentialed young faculty member. Before returning to Howard as a professor in 1965 Lindsey had burnished his 1957 Howard architecture degree with graduate degrees from MIT, one in architecture and the other in city planning.

Upon Lindsey's arrival at HGSD as a professor in August of 1968, he was given a green light to immediately hand pick two recent Howard architecture graduates to enter the HGSD master's program. Lindsey picked a classmate, Michael Amos, and me. Harvard offered both of us a full expenses stipend. That was an offer I couldn't refuse. The "revolution" in DC would have to wait. A Harvard architecture master's degree was an instant ticket to a tenure track faculty position at any HBCU based architecture program and probably several other non-HBCU programs. I left DC in January 1969 for Cambridge, Mass. with my budding young scientist-wife and our one-year old son Marcus.

I joined an eclectic (and mostly white and male) group of bright, energetic, and ambitious people from across the country and several other nations. By the end of the first month in the program I had personally assessed that I fell right in the middle range of ability and intellect of this group of thirty people, despite my clear "affirmative action"-based admission to Harvard.

I left Harvard in June of 1970 with my masters in architecture degree. I immediately walked into a faculty position at the new Federal City College (eventually the University of the District of Columbia). During that year my old Howard University architecture school dean retired. Howard decided that then HGSD architecture professor Jerome Lindsey was the best choice for becoming the next Howard architecture dean. Lindsey left Cambridge and arrived back on Howard's campus in the summer of 1971 and immediately called Michael Amos and me and made both of us job offers as assistant professors.

By the following August of 1972 I became a licensed architect and immediately hung out my shingle as Melvin Mitchell Architects, PC. Within five years my three old 2MJQ buddies Casey Mann, Robert Jayson, and Harry Quintana would join the firm as partners. The combination of being a practicing architect and a uni-

5.13 Carey Jenkins, ca 1976.
Source: Wikipedia Commons

5.14. Martin Luther King, Jr. main hospital building/Drew Medical Center, Watts-Los Angeles.ca 1976. Source: Author.

versity professor was the achievement that I had been dreaming about since arriving at Howard a decade earlier as a 23-year-old army veteran beginning as a freshman in the architecture program.

During that time, I had occasion to renew my ties with my hometown of Los Angeles. Even though I had strong roots in DC, I was still looking for a way to return to Los Angeles as a name partner in an established black-owned firm. My idol, Paul Williams, had retired, so I affiliated my small DC practice with the substantial practice of African American architect Carey Jenkins.

Jenkins was a joint venture partner in the just opened massive Martin Luther King Hospital in the heart of my old Watts neighborhood. Jenkins's black "godfather" was Ted Watkins, a wily old labor union warrior.

Watkins and his powerful Watts Community Labor Action Committee was a well-oiled political machine that had the allegiance of powerful Los Angeles County Supervisor Ernest Hahn. Supervisor Hahn was the white godfather to the black South-Central Los Angeles business community. The new MLK Hospital was being built on the site of the old Palm Lanes public housing project near where I had grown up. Jenkins had to begin the first phase—a $40 million intake-care wing—as part of a three-way joint venture with two other large white architectural firms. Jenkins (with Watkins's and Hahn's help) got contracts to design most of the remaining half-dozen support structures on the site as the sole design architect and Architect of Record.

5.15. By 1978, the 1968 2MJQ Black Advocate Planners had become Melvin Mitchell Architects PC, a downtown DC 20-person architectural firm with Casey Mann, left, myself, Robert Jayson, and Harry Quintana as the principals. Source: Author

By 1976 I had formally joined up with Jenkins. I turned my DC practice into a branch office of his Los Angeles and St. Louis, MO based firm. I talked Jenkins and his St Louis partner, Charles Fleming into also opening an Atlanta, GA office headed by Lafayette Beamon, another old Los Angeles architect-friend who had relocated to Atlanta. Jenkins and Fleming were both very astute businessmen. The affair proved to be an ill-fated three-year adventure that had to be completely abandoned. In January 1979 Marion Barry became the duly elected mayor of Washington, DC and I resumed my DC practice under my own name.

Like any other young architect, I wanted to work on exciting high-profile projects that would showcase my talents. My marketing strategy with Barry's administration worked. I spent the first year of his tenure working on dirty, unprofitable inspection work. For the next several years after that, I had all of the housing design contracts I could handle. So did several other perceptive young upstart black firms, including the Paul Devrouax and Marshall Purnell partnership. Barry and his housing director had identified my firm and the Devrouax firm as savvy young players who had departed from the "uptown" location in the heart of black DC on Georgia Avenue, long favored by most of the more established black firms. Our two firms each opened new offices on upscale Connecticut Avenue in the "golden triangle" business district in Northwest DC. We were channeling the Bryant & Bryant firm that had been on the Avenue all alone for over a decade. We quickly established an image with the Barry brain trust as the "slick downtown Connecticut Avenue crew."

The 1978-88 decade was a very fruitful, exciting, and profitable time for my practice. Much like a number of other black-owned practices around the country in big cities headed by Black Power-minded mayors, my firm underwent the

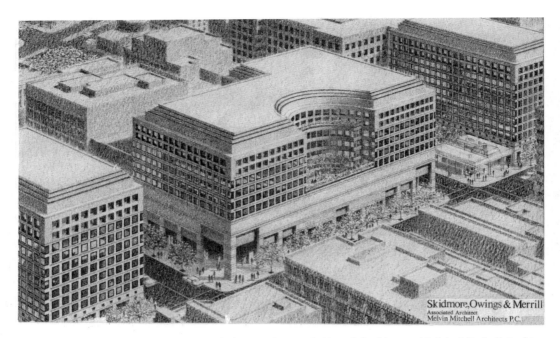

5.16 Metro Center, Washington DC. Skidmore Owens & Merrill Architects, Melvin Mitchell Architects PC, Associated Architect, ca 1981.
Source: Courtesy of Skidmore Owens & Merrill Architects

well-meaning but awkward experience of being "paired up" on a huge downtown development project. The development teams on such projects were routinely all white affairs. But these deals always required massive assistance from city governments. Mayors like Barry had the audacity to say to lead developers something like "if you are going to need my approvals on anything in order to make your project numbers work financially—zoning relief, city owned land costs write downs and so on—put some black people, developer partners, lawyers, contractors, architects, whatever, on your team."

My "associated architect" adventure came on a new one million square foot mixed use office-hotel-retail project situated at the geographic heart of downtown DC. Sitting atop the center of the city's underground rapid transit system, the project was known simply as Metro Center. The developer was DC's premier real estate developer, Oliver Carr. The Carr-Metro Center team was expanded to include Barry's favorite black developer Ted Hagans as Carr's co-developer. Carr's general contractor, local giant Clark Enterprises, paired up with Roger Blount, a highly regarded black contractor. Carr's architect was Skidmore Owens and Merrill, the big international corporate giant known commonly as SOM.

Barry had policies in place that mandated a minimum twenty-five percent slice of the architect portion of the fee. In reality my firm—as the SOM counterpart—was only able to absorb half of that amount over the three-year period of design and construction work. But the steady flow of monthly cash was very much appreciated despite my having to delegate several of my most able staff architects to the SOM office. The ring side seat at the big game of downtown real estate development was a valuable learning experience. However, I was clear that the "associate architect" thing was not something I wanted to repeat. I pressed on with other projects in our role as prime architect.

Over much of that decade I was on an unplanned hiatus from my true calling as a university architecture professor. I used that time to burnish my credibility as a teacher. My young firm's breakout projects as design architects included the total gut rehabilitation-modernization of two large apartment buildings in the mid-town Columbia Heights section of DC. The first was a 200-unit condo conversion of Envoy Towers for middle-income buyers. The second was the 237-unit Cavalier Apartments for low income renters. Both projects were occupied primarily by African Americans.

The client for each of these two big projects were white developers seeking to ingratiate themselves with the Barry Administration. While completing those two projects we were engaged by the Barry Administration to prepare a master-plan study for the reuse of a dilapidated World War II era barracks-style public housing project in the Anacostia section of DC. In 1988, I was part of a development team that was competitively selected by the city housing department to develop the proposed sixteen acre subdivision of single-family homes portion of the twenty-six acre site.

After two years of planning and securing regulatory and community approvals my developer-client decided that the project was not sufficiently profitable and walked away. The city government asked me to take on the developer's role. The city's request came with an offer to provide me with adequate financing. The opportunity to play the role of architect-developer while also being allowed to

5.17 Envoy Towers condo modernization, ca. 1981 and 5.18 The Cavalier Apartments modernization, ca. 1983. Source: Author

pursue my dream of actually building an all modular factory-built homes project was irresistible. I spent the next decade completing this new 110 homes subdivision. Despite my work as a conventional architect on a variety of projects during my career, this project continues to this day to be my most personally fulfilling professional accomplishment. The project was—as hoped for by the city housing department—a catalyst for thousands of additional new single-family homes and walk-up apartment projects for low to moderate income black families in a part of DC that previously had been long neglected by private investment capital.

While preparing to break ground on our Knox Hill Subdivision another former Howard architecture school classmate and aspiring young developer, Harry Calhoun, engaged us to design our largest project, Mount Vernon Plaza. This was a new 250-unit high-rise and townhouse apartment complex sitting on an acre of vacant land on the edge of downtown DC. The multi-million-dollar project required the help of several former Howard classmates and friends who were working high up in the Barry housing administration.

5.19 Setting factory-built modular boxes on foundations at the project site, ca. 1994. Source: Author.

5.20 Author standing in foreground at the entrance to the completed 110-unit single-family subdivision at Knox Hill Village, Washington, DC, ca. 1996. Source: Author.

Calhoun lost control of the project and had to bring in a large new developer. My new developer-client on the planned Mount Vernon Plaza project was the Bush Organization, a white-owned developer based in Norfolk, Virginia. The company had been my client on the successfully completed Cavalier Apartment modernization project. The Bush people fully accepted my ambition to completely control all architectural design, construction supervision, engineering consultant selections, and fee disbursements . In situations like this one, a new developer usually brings in their favorite large (and virtually always white) architectural firm

5.21 Vacant one-acre site at 10th and M Streets, downtown D. C. ca. 1986.
5.22 Model of proposed new building at 10th and M Street. ca. 1988.
5.23 Completed Mount Vernon Plaza Apartment Project, 10th and M Street. Ca 1990.
Sources: Author.

and quickly relegates a firm like mine to "associated architect" status despite all of my prior hard work of bringing the project to design feasibility.

I was also able to complete the design and complete construction supervision on several other large public housing and public-school modernization projects during this period. That 1980-90 decade ended in a time of national recession. During the third Barry term in 1990 the DC government was in the throes of a financial meltdown, and African American architectural firms were in crisis just like every other business. By the close of the 1990s, Barry and the old Black Power crowd from the late 1960s to early 1970s had lost control of or influence over the financial reins of the DC government.

That control and eventually the entire government would pass to the "civic minded–good government" mayors. Sharon Pratt Kelly came first and was succeeded by Anthony Williams. Although an African American, Williams appeared indifferent to the Black Power–black nationalist zeitgeist Barry had been committed to. After several years in power, however, Williams revealed a sophisticated attitude toward black power that was not readily apparent during the early months of his administration.

In 1986 I was hired by Clarence Pearson, Jr. an old acquaintance and architect-professor who had single-handedly built a highly productive two-year architectural technology degree program at the University of the District of Columbia (UDC). The program was a gateway to architectural careers for hundreds of African Americans. Pearson had an even bigger vision: to transform the program into a five-year professional degree program and establish an innovative companion on-campus clinic practice. I was squarely on board with his vision. In 1988 I had completed the restructuring of my professional life around full-time teaching. I kept my hand in public life by accepting several Barry appointments

5.24 Mount Vernon Plaza Project, M Street elevation at duplex units and midrise wing. ca. 1992. Source: Author

to the Board of Registrars and Examiners of Architects (later shortened to the Board of Architecture), and the powerful but contentious Historic Preservation Review Board.

I left UDC in 1995 and in 1997 became the director of the still fledgling (but fully accredited) architecture program at HBCU-Morgan State University in Baltimore. My five-year term in that position was the most fulfilling academic achievement of my life. During that time at Morgan I found the time to write my first book, *The Crisis of the African American Architect.*

In 1999 I made my first trip back to what many black people call the *real* old country. My two-week stay in the West African nation of Ghana was nothing short of a personal religious experience. In 1957, Ghana was the first black state to achieve independence from a European colonial power. I went to Ghana with a vague notion that this was the African nation that should be Zion for Black Americans (rather than Liberia as was assumed 120 years earlier).

I was determined that my first trip to Africa would be via Ghana Airways, the national airline. I just assumed that Europeans were flying the airplanes in their modern fleet of American-made machines. One of the many little details that I was unaware of was that on a trans-oceanic flight of over six hours, international flight regulations required two cockpit crews, or a total of six pilots with at least two captains, aboard the flight.

So, on the big day of my arriving at the Ghana Airways terminal at JFK Airport in

5.25 Boarding Ghana Airways DC-10 aircraft, JFK to Accra, ca. 1999. Source: Author.
5.26 One of the Ghana Airways DC-10 aircraft captains

New York, I went from having never seen a black airline captain in the cockpit of a jumbo jet to seeing an all-black cockpit crew roll up to board and take command of the giant Ghana Airways DC-10 aircraft being refueled for the journey back to the old country.

I shifted my curiosity to the handful of white passengers boarding our plane. Either this (for me) earth-moving event was not registering with the white passengers, or they were doing a hell of a good job of faking no concern. Needless to say, the nine-hour flight, mostly spent suspended 35,000 feet above the Atlantic Ocean, was no different from the countless cross-country flights I had made back and forth between DC and Los Angeles on American DC-10 airliners.

There were many intoxicating sights, sounds, and activities around the big capital city of Accra. So also, for the smaller Ashanti capital at Kumasi, the campus of the Kumasi University of Science and Technology, and in the industrial port twin cities of Secondi–Takoradi. Ghana had a growing chorus of architects who were trained in the architecture school at Kumasi and overseas in Russia, Great Britain, Canada, and the United States. The Ghanaian architects were all committed international-style modernists. They were all "little Le Corbusiers." Ghanaian architects did not appear in the least bit interested in post-modern architecture or any other form of European or American historicism or theory–*thank goodness!* From high-rise buildings in downtown Accra to the new rural village homes of successful sons and daughters, there were poured-in-place concrete buildings under construction everywhere.

The Ghanaian architects emulated the Le Corbusier of the early 1920s, when his work was all straight lines and planes. Though Picasso-Cubism inspired, this work was not yet as openly black African–inspired as Le Corbusier's mid-1950s design of the Ronchamp Chapel in France, or the new Indian city of Chandigarh. The Ghanaian architect's predilection for the use of poured-in-place concrete was on full display throughout the city.

The 1990s Ghanaian architectural educators and professionals all operated within the same mind set of their American counterparts on the subject of the architect's role in the larger building culture. The assumption is that the architect is supposed to react to government patrons and wealthy private clients on what is to be built, why it is to be built, and for whom. Given the rigidly reactionary Eurocentric mindset of these two client prototypes, this line of thinking has led to the same crisis confronting American architects generally and African American architects acutely.

I completed my sojourn of leading the Morgan program in 2002. In the following year I returned to the UDC faculty as adjunct professor of architecture. In 2004, I began another partnership with an old mentor, Charles Bryant. I believed at that time that his forty-year-old legacy architectural firm, Bryant & Bryant, was a good vehicle for the next chapter of my professional life. That year, the two of us corporately merged our two firms to created Bryant Mitchell, PLLC, with Charles Bryant as president-CEO. Within one year, Bryant died suddenly of a massive heart attack while at work in our office. I spent the next dozen years as president/CEO of Bryant Mitchell, PLLC. Much of that time was spent in a close working relationship that I forged with the Alexandria, Virginia, office of Fanning-Howey Architects, a large Midwest-based architecture firm that specialized in public school design work. I ended that relationship right after the August 2015 completion of a multi-million-dollar modernization and addition to a DC public school project for special needs students (below Figure 5.27).

In my role as prime contractor and Architect of Record, I am able to say that the project was an aesthetic and community success. The project was also a very valuable learning experience in public-sector fast-track design–build project management. Financially the project was a disaster. Despite a low seven figure design contract my firm ended up with a low six figure loss at the close out of the project. To reach profitability my small firm would have had to do at least one – possibly several more similar projects of this magnitude and in succession for the same public agency client. However, I had made up my mind that I did not have a passion for this type of work. I was at a point in my life of being determined to change direction and embrace my true intertwined passions of teaching for several more years, providing consulting services to younger but promising developers, and writing several more books on the future of professional practice for African American architects.

In February of 2016, I returned to Howard's architecture program in what turned out to be a very personally and professionally fulfilling two-year appointment as James E. Silcott Professor, an endowed chair in the architecture program. That year I also began reprising the role I had played nearly three decades earlier on my breakout Mount Vernon Plaza apartment project. The planned Renaissance Plaza housing development (next page 70, Figure 5.29) is nearly the same size as my 1990-completed Mt. Vernon Plaza project (page 65, Figures 5.21, 5.22 and 5.23).

My developer-client back then on Mount Vernon already had a wealth of experience, having completed more than a dozen projects that were in the same size range as Mount Vernon. The combination of financing tools I had been ex-

5.27 Rendering of the proposed design for the River Terrace Education Center, NE Washington, DC, a DC public school project. The project was completed in late 2015.
Source: Bryant Mitchell-FHAI joint venture office, Alexandria, VA.

5.28 A partial gathering of architecture faculty, students, and alumni in front of the Mackey Building, College of Engineering & Architecture, Howard University, Washington, DC, ca 2017. Author is standing second from right, front row: Source: Author

posed to back then were still applicable today with a few update twists. Today my young African American developer-client group is moving towards breaking ground on the Renaissance housing and retail deal through the utilization of the same financing structures and sources.

Another one of my young developer-clients is aggressively re-visiting a professional practice business model that I first ventured on thirty years earlier when I assumed the responsibility of developing the 110-unit Knox Hill Village housing subdivision in Southeast DC. The state of the art of modular building today has advanced ten-fold since I began pursuing the modular housing idea.

5.29. Proposed Renaissance Gateway mixed-use residential and retail project rendering at Old Central Avenue, Capitol Heights, Maryland. Source: Author

6. *African American Architects in Current Practice* (1991): The Jack Travis Book   Revisited

In the late 1980s, Harlem-based Jack Travis was the first serious and relatively well-known African American practitioner who openly combined the words *black*, *blackness*, and *black culture* with the word *architecture*. His clients and commissions laid to rest the dread that a *black architecture* would be a devalued architecture. His work and his teaching, writing, advocacy, and organizing across the global black diaspora during the past forty years have been essential and clarifying. In 1991, Travis published his book *African American Architects in Current Practice.*

Travis profiled two dozen black-owned architecture firms and their thirty-four founding owners. The book also provided a brief profile of two prominent architect-academics. The Travis book hit with an impact not felt since a November 1958 issue of *Ebony* that featured eighteen young African American architects (see chapter 5). He profiled practices located in key cities that had come under the control of strong-willed black mayors. The mayors controlled the public agencies that became a disproportionately large source of design contracts in African American architect-owned practices. These agencies relied on scarce public funds that left little room for the spectacular gestures usually found in the projects featured in mainstream architectural magazines, which showcase mostly white male elite architects.

Travis was, on balance, remarkably prescient in his choices of the firms and their owners. Out of the thirty-four architects Travis profiled, twenty-seven went on to elevation to the prestigious American Institute of Architects College of Fellows. Travis was included in this group for his two decades of pathfinding work of embracing an underlying black culture-based aesthetic in a presumptively "white" American architecture. One of the profiled principals went on to become the first black president of the AIA national organization.

Whether deliberately or merely coincidentally, four of his choices had appeared thirty-three years earlier in the *Ebony* article. The *Ebony* article estimated that in 1958 there was a total of "100 licensed Negro architects" in the U.S. out of a total of 20,000 licensed American architects at that time.

In the 1991 Travis book the total number of black licensed architects in the U.S. had grown to 800 out of a total of 40,000 licensed American architects. Nine of the twenty-four firms profiled in 1991 continue to this day as highly re-

6.1 Jack Travis, ca. 2017.
Source: Courtesy of Jack Travis Architect

garded niche players in regional markets. Deaths and the absence of either suc-cession plans or appropriate growth strategies account for the fate of the rest.

In hindsight in 1991 there were several noteworthy black-owned architectural firms that were not in the Travis book. The founding owners of two of those firms are today arguably the number one and two ranked African American architects in the entire nation (one, Phil Freelon, is recently deceased; the other is Curtis Moody who is still very much alive and in full command of his firm). In the follow-ing pages of this chapter, we will revisit eight of twenty-four profiled firms. Four of the eight were repeaters from the November 1958 *Ebony* article. We will also look at the two architect-academics profiled by Travis in 1991.

We began here, as did Travis in his 1991 book, with J. Max Bond, Jr. (1935-2009). In that year Bond was already being declared in many quarters as the dean of the entire corps of African American architects. By the time of his death in February of 2009 Bond was unarguably the most well-known and respected living African American architect in the nation among white academics, the professional practice establishment, and other critical authority figures.

In 1964 Bond, with his Harvard Graduate School of Design and Harvard under-graduate degrees in hand, left the U.S. to spend two years teaching and practicing in the newly independent West African nation-state, Ghana. While there Bond es-tablished his credentials as a Le Corbusier modernist with his design of a library in the Bolgatanga region of Ghana.

6.2 J. Max Bond, Jr. ca. 1990.
Source: Courtesy of Jack Travis Architect

6.3 Bolgatanga Library, Ghana Republic ca 1965. Source: Wikipedia Commons

Bond brought jaw-dropping credentials and credibility to an always skeptical Harlem when he returned New York City from Ghana in 1966. Shortly after arriving he became director of the Architects Renewal Committee of Harlem (ARCH). After leaving ARCH in the early 1970s Bond established an orthodox architectural practice, Bond Ryder Architects, with New York architect Donald Ryder.

In the late 1970s Bond Ryder was handpicked by the King Family to design the Martin Luther King, Jr. Center for Nonviolent Social Change. The Center opened in 1981 and soon became one of the most iconic buildings in all of Black America.

6.4. MLK, Jr. Center for Nonviolent Social Change, Atlanta, ca. 1982. Source: Wikipedia Commons
6.5 Schomburg Center for Research in Black Culture. Source: Wikipedia Commons

From there, Bond's stature continued to grow. He also designed the building modernization that resulted in the Schomburg Center for Research in Black Culture. The Schomburg sits at the geographic center of Harlem, New York City. In addition to his practice, Bond also became a professor and eventually chair of the architecture department at Columbia University. He went on to become dean of the architecture school at City University of New York, and a member of the New York City Planning Commission. In 1990, the prominent Jewish-owned, New York City–based Davis and Brody Architects restructured the firm with Bond as a name partner.

In 2006, Bond, and his firm Davis Brody Bond, began collaborating with Phil Freelon on pre-design and programming studies for a new African American history and culture museum in Washington, DC. In 2008, Bond and Freelon added David Adjaye to their team's pursuit of the contract to design the project. Freelon, Adjaye, Bond (with the Smith Group as production and construction administration lead), was selected in 2009. FAB, as the team became known, bested an A-list of world-class architectural firms. The NMAAHC opened in September 2016 on the National Mall in Washington, DC

Charles McAfee (1925-) and Cheryl McAfee of Wichita and Atlanta, was one of the father-daughter teams featured by Travis in 1991. The two of them were joined by architect-daughter Charyl McAfee-Duncan. Charles McAfee has lived a prolific professional life of compiling "firsts" since his graduation from architecture school and launching his firm in the early 1960s. By 2000 McAfee was regarded in a number of influential quarters as being the most consequential African American architect in the nation, despite the many counter arguments of Max Bond as the dean of the nation's black architects.

McAfee and his daughters have amassed an enviable body of large award-winning projects. The firm oversaw the design and construction of billions of dollars of work in the preparation of the city of Atlanta for the 1996 Olympics. The firm

6.6 Charles McAfee
Source: Courtesy of
Jack Travis Architect

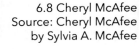
6.7 Cheryl McAfee
ca 1990. Sources:
Courtesy of
Jack Travis Architect

6.8 Cheryl McAfee
Source: Cheryl McAfee
by Sylvia A. McAfee

6.9 Charyl McAfee.
Source: Wikipedia
Commons

6.10 Charyl McAfee
Source: Charyl McAfee

Jesse Jackson
Helps Dedicate
Inner-City
Modular Housing
Plant in Kansas

(L-R) President & CEO Charles McAfee, Marketing
Director Gail Finney and the Rev. Jesse Jackson at
reception celebrating the grand opening of modular
home producer McAfee Mfg. in Wichita, KS.

6.11 McAfee opening McAfee Manufacturing modular housing plant, ca. 1994.
Source: Author and courtesy of Modular Homebuilding Magazine

was also lauded for the design of Atlanta's largest rapid transit station and a leadership role in the modernizing of the city's world-class airport.

However, McAfee's pioneering 1970s actions in providing affordable home ownership for black inner-city families may prove to be his most consequential work. MacAfee joined forces with several other black business entrepreneurs in the launching of a modular housing plant in his home town of Wichita, KS. Typically, the risk and debt capital required to sustain that venture was just not forthcoming at that time. In 1994, McAfee re-initiated his earlier revolutionary housing thrust. He again founded and operated an inner city-based modular housing plant. This time around the plant's grand opening and dedication was the cover story in the January 1995 issue of *Automated Builder Magazine*. Unfortunately, McAfee's boldness and vision were still unable to overcome his lack of access to the necessary levels of financial capital required to sustain that operation. McAfee has paved a path that still must be taken up and brought to realization by a new generation of African American architect-entrepreneurs.

McAfee retired in 2006. Leadership of his firm McAfee3 is in the hands of his daughters Cheryl and Charyl. Both McAfee daughters received masters in architecture degrees from the Harvard Graduate School of Design. Both daughters also followed in their father's footsteps in becoming members of the AIA College of Fellows. This father and two daughters trio is the only one of its kind in the entire 160-year history of the AIA.

The firm has expanded beyond Wichita and Atlanta with an office in Dallas, Texas. The McAfee3 firm today appears to be configured for a continuation as a niche firm with a highly diverse client mix of public sector agencies, institutions, and corporate clients.

Harry Simmons Jr. (1944-1994), a Brooklyn-based architect, was a classmate of mine at Howard University. Simmons was also a close personal friend. He was mentioned in a depressing 1994 *New York Times* article by David Dunlap. The

6.12 Harry Simmons Jr. ca 1990. Source: Courtesy of Jack Travis Architect

6.13 Percy Ifill and Conrad Johnson. Source: Courtesy of Roberta Washington.

6.14 Harlem State Office Building, ca 2010. Source: Author

Dunlap article—lamenting the woes of African American practitioners—appeared just two years before a lengthy *Times* article by famed critic Herbert Muschamp. The Muschamp article effusively extolled the brilliance and hegemony of Jewish American architects in American architecture. Simmons' life, his work, and his relationship to the Brooklyn and Harlem communities was nearly the exact opposite of every negative thing reporter Dunlap had written about the plight of African American architects.

Simmons began his New York career as a designer in the office of a then prominent black-owned New York firm, Ifill and Johnson (Percy Ifill and Conrad Johnson are both deceased). Their thirty person firm was the Architect of Record for the Adam Clayton Powell Harlem State Office Building that anchors the corner of 125th Street and Lenox Avenue (Malcolm X Boulevard) in Harlem.

The building opened in 1973. The actual design of the constructed building was the work of Harry Simmons, who was also then a recent Pratt Institute master's in architecture program graduate.

Credit for the dual fact of the massive project being built in the center of Harlem and being designed by a black-owned firm belongs to the legendary U.S. Congressman Adam Clayton Powell, Jr. The project is a literal monument to Powell and his willingness to exercise his audacious black power.

A young Simmons was eerily prophetic in a September 16, 1979 New York Times article when asked to comment on the struggles facing aspirant black firms; "You can't emulate white architects and survive." The core of Simmons' practice was federal, state, and locally subsidized housing for low-moderate and middle-income black New York City dwellers. Simmons had a lengthy roster of community-based nonprofits and for-profits that acted as sponsor-developers of his projects. He made himself the consummate expert in ways to deliver those projects through the sluggish New York City municipal bureaucracy. Without a hint of vanity, he once candidly made the following remark to me;

> Mitch, I put a lot of money in a lot of my people's hands ... young kids, college students, young aspiring architects, older down on their luck architects, laborers, skilled tradesmen, suppliers, subs, contractors, real estate agents, the arts community, the banks, and on and on ... and of course my family is well taken care of.

Simmons offered me his most prescient brotherly advice during my early 1980s total dependence on government agency contracts: "Mitch, I have serious concerns about all of those DC government contracts your practice seems to be built around."

Simmons fulfilled much of his promise with his Brooklyn-based home office practice. He designed and oversaw the completion of thousands of affordable multifamily apartment buildings and brownstones across the city. Simmons was also, at the insistence of his deep base of community supporters, awarded the commission to design a new wing of Brooklyn's Medgar Evers Community College. Simmons never wavered about his early decision establishing his practice on the ground floor of a Brooklyn brownstone residence. He also bought and rented out other brownstones throughout his neighborhood. Simmons' "home office" modus operandi is an object lesson that in today's world a home-based office (that you actually own) is always a winning strategy for a small firm.

In that 1979 *New York Times* article Simmons remarked that he is so enthusiastic about his work that "I sound like a real Southern preacher." He went on in the article to say that his excitement carries over into his desire to open up his townhouse to community groups for art exhibitions and meetings. In 1994, just fifteen years later, his life was tragically cut short in the fiery crash of his beloved twin-engine airplane.

Roberta Washington (1945–) of New York City, is a product of Howard University's architecture program and Columbia University's master's program. She was one of a group of twenty-four black men and women admitted to the Columbia program during the late 1960s time of national turmoil. She established her practice in 1983 in the heart of a bustling New York

6.15 Roberta Washington, ca 1990. Source: Courtesy of Jack Travis Architect

6.16 Roberta Washington, ca 2015. Source: Courtesy of Roberta Washington Architect.

6.17 1400 5th^h Ave, New York, Roberta Washington Architects, ca. 2003.
Source: Courtesy of Roberta Washington Architect.

city neighborhood. Her practice, at that time, was one of the few black woman-owned architectural firms in the nation.

The firm's primary work is in the design of health care facilities, educational facilities, and affordable multifamily apartment buildings. Washington was a past board member of the New York Coalition of Black Architects (NYCOBA). By 1991 when she was featured in the Jack Travis book Washington had established an impressive young practice.

Since that year, her career and practice has flourished. She has won numerous design and community service awards and other "firsts" as a pioneering black female practitioner. She became the first woman president of the National Organization of Minority Architects (NOMA). Today Washington continues to head her small niche housing and education facilities practice. The 660-student Bernard Environmental Magnet School in New Haven, Connecticut and the 128-unit mid-rise condo—Harlem's first green and smart building—at 1400 5th Avenue are representative of the many projects her small practice continues to produce.

Washington has been able to groom a succession line of in-house management that is allowing her to devote more of her time to writing, teaching, and her passion for mentoring a next generation of minority women practitioners.

Robert Madison (1923-) in 1991 was already a prolific and distinguished practitioner and pioneering figure in Ohio. Madison was also featured thirty-three years earlier in the 1958 *Ebony* magazine article. In 1960 he opened the first African American-owned architectural practice in the state of Ohio.

Madison has played a design role in many prestigious projects that include U.S. embassies, the Cleveland Browns Stadium, Horseshoe Casino, the Louis Stokes Wing at Cleveland Public Library, and the Rock and Roll Hall of Fame. Madison

6.18 Robert Madison, ca 1990. Source: Courtesy of Jack Travis Architect

6.19 Sandra Madison, ca 2016. Source: Wikipedia Commons

is a former Howard University professor as well as holder of an honorary doctorate from Howard. His firm, Madison International, Inc., continues in operation under the leadership of a second generation of Madisons. His daughter-in-law, architect Sandra Madison is now the CEO of the firm with her architect-husband Kevin, Robert Madison's son. The twenty person niche firm is currently serving the state of Ohio on a variety of building types and services.

6.20 Norma Sklarek, ca 1990. Source: Courtesy of Jack Travis Architect

6.21 Norma Sklarek, ca 2010. Source: Wikipedia Commons

Norma Sklarek (1926-2012) was already the pioneering first lady of black women architects in the U.S in 1991. She was the third black female to receive an architect license in the U.S. and the first to be inducted into the AIA College of Fellows. Sklarek was also featured in the November 1958 EBONY article. Sklarek graduated from Columbia in 1950 and worked as a designer at SOM, the giant modernist commercial office building design firm in New York City. In the early 1960s Sklarek headed to Los Angeles to work for Victor Gruen Associates, an international powerhouse firm credited with the design of major enclosed shopping malls. She moved from Gruen to the position of managing partner in several other high-profile offices that included Cesar Pelli and John Jerde. Sklarek continued to be a leading light in the profession and major role model and mentor for black and white women in architecture right up to the time of her death in 2012.

John Chase (1925-2012), through a U.S. Supreme Court ruling in 1950 enrolled in the University of Texas School of Architecture. This was a first at a traditionally-white, deep-south architecture program. Chase was a trail blazing Houston-based practitioner who first appeared 33 years earlier in the 1958 *Ebony* magazine article on young black architects.

6.22 John Chase, ca 1990. Source: Courtesy of Jack Travis Architect.

6.23 John Chase, ca 2010. Source: Wikipedia Commons

In 1971, Chase joined with eleven other black practitioners to found the National Organization of Minority Architects. Large black churches and residences were the base of Chase's early years of practice in Houston. By 1991 when he was profiled by Travis, his firm was working on large new building design commissions from HBCU-Texas Southern University and other similar publicly funded institutions. That work was followed by other major public sector funded projects, and private commercial work. He grew his Houston firm to 50 persons with branch offices in three other cities. Though his firm no longer exists, several of his earlier senior vice presidents went on to head their own practices.

Louis Fry, Sr. (1903-2000) and Louis Fry, Jr. (1929-2006) were the first black father-son duo to hold concurrent AIA Fellow status. Louis Fry, Jr. was featured thirty-three years earlier in the inspiring Ebony Magazine article on black architects. The firm initially operated as Fry and Welch, a legacy firm that was founded in 1954 by Fry Sr. who was also a highly influential professor in the Howard University School of Engineering & Architecture from 1952 until his retirement in 1972. Fry Jr. joined the firm in early 1960s. The firm designed numerous substantial projects that included HBCU institutions across the South, large public housing projects, public schools, and private sector funded multifamily housing projects in Washington, DC and Maryland.

6.24 Louis Fry, Sr., Louis Fry, Jr., and Louis Fry, III, ca 1990. Source: Courtesy of Jack Travis Architect

Louis Fry III left the firm after his father's death in 2006 to join a black-owned DC firm, Lance Baily & Associates. Fry, III reopened the firm in 2012 as Fry and Welch Associates, PC, a non-profit ministry that provides consulting professional services to religious congregations.

The Architect-Academics

6.25 Sharon Sutton, ca 1990. Source: Courtesy of Jack Travis Architect

6.26 Sharon Sutton, ca 2015. Source: Wikipedia Commons

Sharon Sutton (1941-) is a 1973 Columbia University architecture graduate who also earned Ph.D. in psychology in 1982. In 1976 she was the twelfth African American woman to be licensed to practice architecture in the U.S. By 1991 she had risen to the rank of tenured associate professor of architecture at the University of Michigan.

She was the first black woman to be promoted to full professor of architecture at a traditionally-white university architecture program (1994), and the second to be elected a Fellow in the American Institute of Architects (1995). From 1996-2016 Sutton amassed a prodigious body of work in design research and community activism while a professor in the School of Architecture at the University of Washington in Seattle.

Sutton is author of the book *When Ivory Towers Were Black: A Story about Race in America's Cities and Universities (2017)*. She also wrote *Weaving a Tapestry of Resistance: The Places, Power and Poetry of a Sustainable Society (1996)*. She has authored numerous book chapters and journal articles. Sutton has returned to New York City and is currently adjunct distinguished professor at Parsons.

6.27 Harry G. Robinson, ca 1990. Source: Courtesy of Jack Travis Architect

6.28 Harry G. Robinson, ca 2017. Source: Courtesy of Harry G. Robinson, III

Harry G. Robinson, III (1944-) was arguably the most consequential black architect in academia in the nation in 1991 when profiled by Travis. He is a graduate of Howard University's School of Engineering and Architecture, and the Harvard Graduate School of Design.

In 1991 he was dean of the Howard University

School of Architecture and Planning. Under Robinson's leadership between 1979-1995 the Howard program continued the legacy established by Robinson's mentor Howard H. Mackey.

Under Robinson the architecture program continued to be one of the largest producers of black architects who would graduate, attain licensure, and eventually go on to found architectural practices. These Howard-trained architects are in Washington, DC, other cities across the nation, and across the global Diaspora space.

Robinson's consummate communications skills gave the Howard program as well as the nation's black architects a high level of visibility during his reign. His illustrious career was filled with barrier-breaking appointments over the course of his term as dean. He was the first African American chairman of the United States Commission of Fine Arts that he served on from 1994 to 2003, first African American president of the National Architectural Accrediting Board, first African American president of the National Council of Architectural Registration Boards, and first African American executive consulting architect for the American Battle Monuments Commission.

After voluntarily stepping down as dean in 1995 he was appointed as Howard's Interim Vice President for Academic Affairs. Shortly after that assignment he was named as Vice President for University Administration. In that role he guided the University through the process of producing a new campus master plan. During that time Robinson co-authored with Hazel Edwards a very influential book titled *The Long Walk: The Placemaking Legacy of Howard University (1996)*–(Edwards is the current head of the architecture program at Howard). In 1997, he left administrative duties and returned to the architecture program in a teaching role as James E. Silcott Professor of Architecture. He also returned to managing his busy international urban design practice.

In his role as professor over the following two decades, Robinson was instrumental in recruiting a series of successor leaders of the architecture program. In 2016 his guidance and counsel resulted in the faculty's unanimous selection of Hazel Edwards as the first woman chair of the architecture program in its 100 years of existence.

Robinson retired in 2017 and retains his title as Professor and Dean Emeritus, School of Architecture and Planning, Howard University (in 1995 the School of Architecture and Planning was re-merged with the School of Engineering to form the College of Engineering and Architecture).

In concluding this review of a select number of the firms and entities featured in the Jack Travis 1991 book, *African American Architects in Current Practice*, one cannot resist the lure of hindsight. There clearly were more firms doing substantive work in other cities that year. Given the additional resources, the two dozen practitioners Travis profiled could have been easily expanded by an equal number of accomplished or promising firms drawn from the two hundred African American architect–owned firms in existence in that year.

Today, nearly three decades since the publication of the Travis book, old age, deaths, and changing conditions have left only nine of those twenty-four showcased architectural practices remaining as on-going operations. Several of those surviving firms appear to have found just the right size and niches among their still mainly public-sector client bases that allow them to remain viable as orthodox fee-for-services architectural firms. However, several of the surviving firms show signs of awareness of their need to rethink their orthodox business models and mindsets. I can sum up the reality that Black America and black architects can never lose sight of thusly:

> Without the passage of civil and voting rights and the election of black mayors and city councilors in the mid-1960s, this entire body of Travis-profiled black architect-designed work would have been awarded to and designed by white-owned architectural firms. Virtually none of this work by black architects was ever published in the architectural press or in contemporary books about architecture.

For the foreseeable future, the overwhelming majority of Black Americans will still live mostly together in urban and nearby suburban communities. If Black America were an independent nation, it would have the tenth-largest gross national income in the world. A "market needs assessment in a competitive environment" is how the entrepreneurial sector of black businesses attempting to serve that market would conceptualize its opportunities. Unfortunately, the orthodox architectural mindset—thus far largely adhered to by black practitioners—does not lead to such a straightforward conceptualization of marketplace opportunities. In retrospect, I believe that the unasked question in 1991 regarding the relatively small and mostly orthodox architectural practices was this:

> What is the appropriate strategic model to be utilized in addressing the physical environment needs of 34 million African Americans in an advanced capitalist, information-age economy?

In 1991, the estimated two hundred black-owned firms were dispersed around the country in much the same way that the rest of the then thirty-four million people in Black America were. Not unsurprisingly, Washington, DC—with a seventy percent majority black population and home to the nation's top black university with a thriving, fully accredited architectural school—had twenty-four of those black-owned firms. Other cities not represented in the Travis book had a number of nominally successful black-owned firms. Seattle on the west coast; Dallas, New Orleans, Nashville, and Miami in the deep south; Columbus and Cincinnati in Ohio; and Pittsburg and Philadelphia in Pennsylvania all fit the description of cities not represented.

The fates of the two hundred black firms around the nation and the twenty-four representative black firms profiled by Travis tracked closely together with difficulties that beset urban Black Americans between 1991 and 2008. Current U.S. Census data shows that Black America's population has grown from thirty-four million in 1990 to forty-four million today—*an increase of over twenty percent*. The growth of black-owned architectural firms is headed in the exact opposite direction. Decreases now exceed a fifty percent *drop*. Between 1980 and today black-owned architectural firms in the U.S. could be likened to the proverbial "canaries in the coal mine." Their firms are the first to die in the changing atmosphere that can no longer support more than a fraction of the number of conventionally structured businesses that once routinely thrived.

It bears repeating that the word *architecture* has a silent but automatic default preface of the word *white*. The same held for the most visibly hyped buildings, the men who designed them, and the people who were the authorized "critics" (mostly cheerleaders who lionize both). Architecture has been a remarkably accurate mirror that reflects the seats of power and prestige in any modern Western society.

American architecture firms have been utilizing a definition of themselves that is fatally flawed on several major counts. One flaw is the failure to come fully to terms with the profoundly disrupting aspects of the late twentieth century information revolution. The other flaw is the still prevailing architecture culture view of housing (and community development) as "not quite *architecture*." The stand-alone signature building remains the obsessive priority of those who lay claim to doing architecture. Architecture culture still views housing as "something builders, contractors, and developers do."

Over the intervening nearly three decades since the publication of the Travis book, the totality of the information technology revolution alongside of business-cycle expansions and contractions have decimated the profession. Those forces have aided the rise of a new set of players willing to offer paying clients things that architects are conditioned to not do. The conditioning begins in academia and is reinforced by the dominant professional organizations. The new players routinely offer their clients guarantees of project costs and time of deliveries. *Those two offers were game changers.*

Those new players labeled themselves with names like "construction manager, design–build contractors, and developers." They rapidly became the choice of corporations, governments, institutions, and individuals who previously entrusted architects with the lead role in the building enterprise. The challenge of gaining access to capital–always problematic for black architects–became nearly insurmountable for much of the majority profession due largely to their business models.

The internet, globalization, and artificial intelligence made it possible for people from around the planet to devise and transmit drawings to US clients at fractions of the cost that American architects are able to. Seemingly suddenly, a conventional architectural firm of less than seventy-five to one hundred persons, complete with all engineering sub-disciplines, could no longer automatically assume to be a financially viable entity.

The scene today in 2019 is that there is only one black-owned architectural firm that fully meets the description of being larger than one hundred persons and economically viable. Today's remaining one hundred black-owned firms are scattered about in the same cities as in 1991. Most employ between five and thirty persons. All of them are either headed for insolvency or are in the process of completely changing their business models. The really good news is that those firms that transform themselves to twenty-first century business models have an exceedingly bright future.

In order to gain better insight about the issues and forces that have been decimating black-owned architectural firms over past forty years, a more in-depth look at several "canaries" and the lone "unicorn" is in order.

7. Four Firms:
Three Canaries and One Unicorn

In 1991–the year of the release of the Jack Travis book *African American Architects in Current Practice*–Washington, DC-based Bryant & Bryant was a fifty-person architectural firm; a colossus in just about any arena of for-profit black owned businesses in that year. A decade earlier in 1981 the firm was laying a legitimate claim to being the largest black-owned architectural firm in the nation. For whatever reasons, Bryant & Bryant was *not* one of the twenty-four professional practices profiled in the Travis book.

In 1991, Washington, DC architectural firm Devrouax & Purnell was nearly fifteen years old and had a twenty-person payroll. The firm was considered to be a very accomplished entity in DC but not yet on the national black stage. D&P *was* profiled in the Travis book.

In 1991, the Raleigh-Durham, North Carolina, firm The Freelon Group was only a year old but had already won several statewide design awards for design proposals for consequential projects on a trajectory of being constructed. The fledgling young firm was, perhaps justifiably, *not* profiled in the Travis book. By 2009, less than two decades later, the Freelon Group was the lead member of the consortium of architectural firms that had won an international competition to design the 400,000 square foot NMAAHC museum. The firm had by that time grown into a perennially award-winning forty-five-person firm. In 2014, the Freelon Group acquisition sale to national giant Perkins+Will was completed. The Freelon Group no longer exists.

In 1991, the Columbus, Ohio, firm Moody/Nolan, Inc.–founded in 1982–was approaching the twenty-five-person mark in size. The firm was *not* one of the twenty-four professional practices profiled in the Travis book. By 2015, Moody/Nolan had morphed into the category of "large practice" (one hundred to six hundred persons). Moody/Nolan was appearing regularly on annually published national listings of the nation's top firms as measured by audited annual fee income and number of staff professionals.

Each of these four firms offers a distinctly cautionary tale about the perils, pitfalls (and potential rewards if done correctly) of orthodox professional practice in the twenty-first century. Each of these four firms used the same orthodox business model but differed substantially in growth and marketing strategies. I refer to the first three of the four firms as "canaries"–as in "canary in the coal mine." The following pages contain a brief description and history of each of the four firms, beginning with the three "canaries" and concluding with the nation's lone "unicorn" architectural firm.

Bryant & Bryant Architects and Planners, Washington, DC

7.1 Robert and Charles Bryant, ca. 1980.
Source: Courtesy of Bryant Mitchell Architects

Charles Irving Bryant (1929–2005) and Robert Bryant (1932–1995) headed a firm that, in relative size and impact, was a forerunner of Moody/Nolan, the nation's large black-owned architectural practice outlier on the scene today. The trajectory of the Bryants in Washington, DC was a national harbinger of the fate of black firms that hued to the conventional "fee for services" design of random buildings as business model.

The Bryant brothers' story began in 1965 when 1957 Howard graduate Charles Bryant opened his office. Bryant broke with long-standing tradition. The small number of black-owned practices in DC were clustered along Georgia Avenue running through the heart of black DC. The Georgia Avenue corridor was the home base of black businesses and professions of every stripe. Mainstream white firms tended to cluster along the fashionable all-white Connecticut Avenue strip. Charles opened his small office on that same Connecticut Avenue strip. His instincts and timing were right on point.

The black majority population of DC had been ruled over for the prior 100 years by openly racist white mayors and southern congressmen. In 1964 President Lyndon Johnson handpicked mayor Walter Washington, a hometown guy and Howard University Law School graduate. Washington was the former New York City housing director. Johnson also handpicked a racially integrated, mostly liberal, Democrat Party-affiliated city council. White agency heads were starting to feel the pressure to open up prevailing all-white government contracting policies.

Within a year of opening his Connecticut Avenue office, Charles Bryant Associates received a modest contract from the DC government to design a small DC public school addition and modernization. I was entering my fourth year at Howard, newly married, and became Bryant's third employee in their small office. I was charged with completing the project design and all deliverables to the client. A succession of increasingly larger contracts followed. Within five years, the firm had completed a half-dozen public schools and a dozen large new housing projects along the 1968 rebellion-scarred lower Georgia Avenue and 14th Street corridors. By 1972, Bryant & Bryant—now including Bryant's younger architect-brother - Robert Bryant—was able to best larger white DC architectural firms for the contract to design a new 300,000 square foot replacement high school for the historic black Dunbar Senior High School.

7.2. Dunbar High School Replacement, ca. 1977. Source: Courtesy of Charles Bryant III.

7.3 The first Dunbar Sr. High School, ca. 1920. Source: Wikipedia Commons

The new structure arose on the demolition ashes of the 1917-built Tudor-style structure that had been designed by the DC municipal architect of that era. The old Dunbar had become known as the greatest Negro high school in the world. Up until the mid sixties that Dunbar was a national symbol of black excellence. By 1968 Dunbar had become a neighborhood school whose population was drawn entirely from a troubled DC area that was becoming increasingly stricken by the ravages of poverty and powerlessness.

The demolition of the old Dunbar structure and replacement by the new 1976 building split Black DC into two warring camps. One side was bitterly opposed to what it viewed as an act of historic desecration of a near sacrosanct symbol. The other camp saw the proposed new aggressively brutalist-style architecture and its open space interior layouts—designed by a black architect that had been selected by black people—as an act of political resistance to white power and black elitism.

Between 1972 and 1981, Bryant & Bryant was the lead architecture firm in the new million-square-foot University of the District of Columbia campus on upper Connecticut Avenue in Northwest DC (known then as Washington Technical Institute). Bryant & Bryant was also the design architect and Architect of Record on ten of the dozen large new buildings on the UDC campus. The Bryant & Bryant office grew to more than fifty persons. The firm was laying legitimate claim to being the largest black-owned architectural firm in the nation. By 1976 The Bryant firm's $2 million in revenue garnered the anchor spot on the that year's annual *Black Enterprise 100* list of the nation's one hundred largest African American-owned companies. As the only architectural firm on this list, that was a very big deal for black architects.

Layered on top of the firm's huge projects with DC public schools, the Federal General Services Administration for UDC, and the DC housing department, there were also large commissions coming from Howard University. The Howard Cancer Research Center was a typical example of the substantive contracts coming out of Howard.

7.4 Washington Technical Institute, 4200 Connecticut Ave., DC (now the University of the District of Columbia) aerial rendering ca 1978. Source: Wikipedia Commons

7.5. UDC, Administration Building from Dennard Plaza, Source: Author

7.6. Howard University Cancer Research Center. Source: Courtesy of Charles Bryant II

The political sources of the design commissions awarded to Bryant & Bryant, as well as the nearly two-dozen other black-owned DC firms, virtually always required other black people with decision-making roles in running government agencies and other forms of quasi-government entities. A number of those black decision-makers were former Howard University classmates of the Bryants and the heads of the black-owned firms.

The decade from 1980 to 1990 was a magical time for the Bryants. But in a complete reversal of fortune, the following close-out decade of the twentieth century exposed the absence of the foundation necessary for maintaining a fifty-person firm and moving beyond one hundred persons that would have been escape velocity territory. Everything that could possibly go wrong actually went wrong. There was a lethal combination of changes in local black politics, national political parties, the death of Robert Bryant, and the inevitable business-cycle downturns.

By 2003, the Bryant & Bryant firm had shrunken to Charles Bryant and five employees. But the firm was still carrying the overhead infrastructure of the once much larger Bryant firm. In that year I had a chance meeting with the still high-spirited, optimistic, and robustly healthy-looking seventy-five year old Charles Bryant. After nearly a year of conversations between the two of us that sometimes stretched deep into the night, I decided to join his firm. (see Chapter 5, Draft Memoir for added details about my now fifteen year odyssey as CEO of Bryant Mitchell, PLLC).

Devrouax & Purnell, Washington, DC

7.7 Paul Devrouax, Marshall Purnell, ca. 1990.
Source: Courtesy of Jack Travis Architect

7.8 Paul Devrouax, Marshall Purnell, ca 2008.
Source: Courtesy of DP Partners

Paul Devrouax (1942–2010) and Marshall Purnell in 1991 headed a small but promising firm with several impressive projects under its belt. The firm was founded in 1976 by Devrouax. The defining moment in the evolution of this firm was in 1978 when Devrouax enticed Purnell to join the fledgling firm. At that time, D&P, as the firm was commonly known, was holding forth in a small Dupont Circle basement office. Their workload was mostly housing rehabilitation design work projects.

Purnell—like Devrouax—was not a Howard graduate. He was a quick-study type who had learned the ropes of local DC politics over his several years spent as a designer in the Georgia Avenue office of Fry & Welch (Louis Fry, Jr. and Louis Fry, Sr.). Purnell left the Frys to work at the American Institute of Architects headquarters as a minority affairs specialist. In 1971 he was instrumental in helping a small group of the most successful African American architect-practitioners from around the country found the National Organization of Minority Architects (NOMA).

The D&P partnership was based on highly complementary strengths. Purnell brought sophisticated design sense, modern management skills, and public-relations savvy. Those skills were very complementary to Devrouax's highly polished political and "rain-making" skills. Their combined strengths would lead them to a series of breakthrough commissions as a black-owned firm. D&P went on to achieve spectacular successes up through the 2007 recession. In 2008, Purnell became the first black president of the American Institute of Architects. In 2010, Devrouax died suddenly from a massive heart attack.

At that time the firm had a thirty-person staff, an out of proportion overhead burden, and was deeply in debt to their engineering consultants and local-federal withholding tax collection agencies. The political winds had shifted on them for many of the same reasons that befell the Bryants a decade earlier. Like the Bryants before them, the firm also suffered devastating and unrecoverable financial blows from the refusal of several recalcitrant DC government agencies to honor large D&P invoices for completed services and deliverables.

By 2014 Purnell left DC to take up a full-time position as Professor of the Practice in the School of Architecture at North Carolina State University. Several second-generation partners continued operation as DP Partners. The Devrouax & Purnell firm without its two hard-charging partners was not the same force by any measure.

To better understand the state of things at the time of Devrouax's untimely death we need go back to the onset of the first Barry administration in 1979. The previous DC mayor's public works director, Colonel Sam Starobin, and his then mainly white technocrats had hired a joint venture headed by the big majority-owned Alexandria, Virginia, firm known as VVKR to design a large and long overdue new municipal center. The team included D&P and Robert Coles, a highly regarded Buffalo, New York, African American architect. Coles had established a high profile in DC through his activism in the locally based American Institute of Architects. Coles was also a University of Minnesota architecture school classmate of VVKR head Randy Vosbeck.

The VVKR/D&P/Robert Coles team's final drawings were completed and paid for by the prior administration by the time Mayor Barry was inaugurated in January of 1979. Barry decided to abandon the project's site location in downtown DC at Judiciary Square, against the advice of his still largely white city planning staff. The site sat atop a rapid transit station stop. Barry then ordered the joint-venture team to reconfigure the design to fit another vacant site located at the corner of 14th and U Streets.

7.9. The Reeves Center, 14th and U Streets, Washington, D. C., ca. 1986.
Source: Courtesy of DP Partners

This long vacant but charred-remains site once held a popular drug store and a variety of other small businesses. The site was also the exact spot from which, twelve years earlier on the night of April 4, 1968, a dashiki-clad Black Power militant named Marion Barry had unsuccessfully tried to help Stokely Carmichael (the late Kwame Touré) divert an angry torch-bearing crowd.

During the redesign process, Devrouax bonded socially and politically with Barry and all of his key lieutenants. D&P took charge of all interior design, space planning, and furnishing fit outs, including Mayor Barry's command center and satellite offices for all of Barry's cabinet members. D&P became to the Barry government the equivalent of what the Bryants once were to the pre–Home Rule Walter Washington government a decade earlier.

In yet another example of D&P's sophisticated thinking, they fully grasped that the renovation work that black firms like theirs had historically survived on was now becoming fashionable and lucrative thanks to a national historic preservation movement. The Barry government was determined to use another large tranche of money to retrofit the old and crumbling DC City Hall building on Pennsylvania Avenue. The building housed the Barry administration, as had been the case for DC governments over the prior generations.

The Barry Administration determined that D&P had by then established sufficient credentials as rehabilitation and preservation experts to justify being selected as prime architects for this project. By the end of Barry's first term, severe money problems forced the cancellation of construction of the D&P designs for City Hall. A decade would pass before T. Conrad Monts (1942-2009), a very clever and politically well-connected black developer, was able to talk a near desperately insolvent DC government into adopting an innovative turnkey fi-

7.10 The District Building (The John A. Wilson Building) on Pennsylvania Ave., NW DC.
Source: Wikipedia Commons

nance-design-build approach to the City Hall project. By that time construction costs had doubled. Monts' new financing source insisted on bringing on a new architect. D&P remained on the design team as "associated architects" to Monts' new architect, Shalom Baranes. In addition to having all project costs covered Monts received a developers fee of $6 million dollars plus all his reimbursable expenses. This modus operandi and business model did not register with the city's architects.

Going into the 1990s with full design credit as the prime architects for several large projects under their belt, D&P was armed with the edge needed to earnestly pursue private developers and large institutional clients who build large downtown projects. The firm got word of a big office complex being planned by a regional branch of a major quasi-government agency. The project site was in a commercial hub just outside of DC. Here again, black professionals in that mostly white-run agency were sitting in the midst of the architect-selection process.

Through their powerful black allies inside that agency, D&P was able to make the "short list," which contained some of the most recognized architectural names in the Washington, DC region. D&P made a convincing case that the firm was equally qualified to do the project as the prime architect. They were eventually selected for this commission. The success of the project led to a similar commission to design a corporate headquarters in Richmond, Virginia, for a regional bank powerhouse. Here, also, the firm was able to count on the support of powerful black corporate-level professionals inside that organization. D&P would be well positioned to take full advantage of their hard-won experience over the prior twenty years.

Barry, as D&P patron saint, had a grand idea. Barry decided to entertain an over-

7.11. The Federal Home Loan Bank, Vienna, Virginia, ca. 1995.
Source: Courtesy of DP Partners

7.12. The Verizon Center, Washington, DC, ca. 1997. Source: Wikipedia Commons

ture he received from Abe Pollin, a member of a successful Washington, DC Jewish family and the franchise owner of the National Basketball Association's Washington Bullets. Pollin wanted to bring the Bullets from his aging Capital Arena in suburban Landover, Maryland, to a downtown DC location. Pollin's offer was that if given a piece of prime downtown city-owned land plus other financial incentives, he would build a new basketball arena and relocate his team to DC. The new Pollin arena would also accommodate the city's ice hockey franchise and provide a place for the popular Georgetown Hoyas basketball team to play.

So, with a $200 million project coming up, where were DC's African American-owned architectural firms in all of this? Again, one would logically think that the Bryants or some consortium drawn from the two-dozen black-owned firms would be in this picture. Only D&P emerged as part of Abe Pollin's design team. That team comprised the de rigueur powerful, white, out of town architectural firm known as Smith Grylls Hinchman of Detroit (now consolidated as the Smith Group). The design team also included the highly respected local white-owned design firm of Keyes Condon Florance (since acquired by the Smith Group).

The D&P firm played a major role in the locally and nationally lauded final design outcome of the MCI Center, formerly known as the Verizon Center, now known as Capital One Arena. Marshall Purnell, along with D&P's top designer, Anthony Brown, were largely responsible for the brilliant exterior façade designs of the huge two-square-block arena.

After nearly twenty years, Republic Development Corporation, a white-owned Georgetown-based firm that had previously used D&P on a small commercial project, came back to the firm in 1997. This time Republic's partners were in hot pursuit of a DC government-owned downtown parcel large enough for the development as a 400,000 square foot commercial office building. Republic

Figure 7.13. Republic Square, completed ca. 2001. Source: Courtesy of DP Partners

figured that D&P—a black-owned architectural firm that combined proven competence with big-league political instincts and top-level connections—would be the perfect choice. This project broke ground in late 2001.

During those same heady times in the mid-1990s, the finely tuned D&P network antennae revealed that the giant Washington, DC–based Potomac Electric Power Company (PEPCO) was going to consolidate its scattered forces. PEPCO wanted to build a 384,000 square foot headquarters in downtown DC. This was not a project that the Barry administration exerted very much leverage over. PEPCO already owned the land, the zoning was "matter of right," and PEPCO had all of the money in the world. D&P was on its own. The firm would have to rely on a now solid track record of several major municipal government commissions. These included a 300,000 square foot downtown DC commercial office building, a 150,000 square foot corporate headquarters in Richmond for a quasi-government agency, an impressive 190,000 square foot office complex in Northern Virginia for the prestigious Federal Home Loan Bank, and several other large completed projects. The two D&P partners were also very savvy realists

They understood that architectural firms that throw their hats in the ring for 384,000 square foot corporate headquarters buildings will usually have at least ten, and often many more, completed projects of a similar or far greater size to flash on the wall in the important "slide show" interview. If a corporate manager selects a household-name architect who fails to deliver, that manager is not necessarily assumed to have exercised poor judgment in having chosen that firm. However, if the manager selects an unknown "dark horse" that fails to deliver *spectacularly*, he or she will have committed a fatal career error. This part of the story ends happily with PEPCO's selection of D&P as the prime and sole architect for the project. The building they designed was completed in mid-

7.14 The Pepco Building, 7th Street, NW Washington, DC.
Source: Courtesy of DP Partners

2002 . . . and was very well received. The cross street that the building faces was renamed as Paul Devrouax Way in 2018.

Upon the 2001 completion and ribbon-cutting ceremonies for the $50 million PEPCO Building, Devrouax & Purnell was no longer just an architecture firm in the marketplace hunting down architectural fee commissions. As chief D&P rainmaker Paul Devrouax had evolved into a consummate "player" and "deal maker." Big white (and black) prospective clients searched him out to become a key member of their strategy teams when structuring complex real estate transactions that required a thorough working knowledge of how business was done in the city.

Mayor Barry had one more giant public works project that he would add to his legacy despite its actual building occurring on his successor's watch. Before Barry left office in 1990 for a four-year hiatus that was divided between jail and a brief reign as the city councilman for Anacostia, he had started plans to build a new replacement convention center.

The new center was badly needed to replace the aging and undersized convention center that had been built during Walter Washington's time in the 1970s. This time around, D&P elected to join forces with Thompson Ventulett & Stainback (TVS), a large white Atlanta firm with a stellar national track record of successful convention center designs. A deal of this magnitude absolutely had to have the participation of a local white-owned design firm as well. TVS and D&P both had strong past working relationships with the highly respected local architect Ted Mariani. The builder would be the same "salt and pepper" joint venture of Clark Construction Company and the black-owned Smoot Company that had built the Pollin arena.

Just as had happened earlier during the design phase of the Verizon Center,

7.15. Walter Washington Convention Center, ca 2008. Source: Courtesy of DP Partners

D&P and TVS engaged in spirited internal office-to-office design competitions for the establishment of basic convention center design layouts and building exteriors. And, again, similar to events that occurred with the Verizon Center, the convention center client representatives consistently chose conceptual layouts and exterior elevations that had been generated by Marshall Purnell and D&P's chief designer Anthony Brown. Paul Devrouax and Marshall Purnell would share equally in giving Washington its two most important civic commercial edifices of the twenty-first century.

There was yet another major design commission high point to occur in that last decade of Paul Devrouax's life. Allen Y. Lew was hired by Barry's successor, Anthony Williams, to build the replacement DC convention center, manage the billion-dollar modernization of DC's public schools, and build the Washington Nationals baseball stadium. Lew was probably D&P's biggest client and benefactor after Marion Barry. Lew is one of the most gifted and respected public-sector managers to have ever served in DC government.

Lew saw firsthand D&P's performance on the new convention center. He subsequently hired D&P to modernize several DC public schools. Lew had to have had a key role in the orchestration and hiring of the design team for the new multi-million-dollar Nationals Park. D&P is credited, with joint billing with Populous (formerly the entertainment facilities studio of St. Louis-based HOK) as architects for the project. Under Lew, the project was completed over a two-year period, straddling the start of design and construction in 2006 and ending in the 2008 grand opening.

In 2008, D&P was commissioned to design a new office building over the DC mass transit station in the heart of the Shaw–U Street neighborhood. Paul Devrouax and Marshall Purnell had succeeded in positioning the firm as one of DC's premier architectural firms, black or white.

7.16. Washington Nationals Stadium, ca 2009. Source: DP Partners.

7.17. Progression Place–United Negro College Fund Headquarters.
Source: Courtesy of DP Partners

In addition to the multitude of huge commissions occurring in the initial decade of the new millennium, in 2008 D&P was part of a team headed by I.M. Pei & Partners that entered the competition to design the planned National Museum of African American History & Culture. The Pei–D&P submission was one of the six finalist firms whose full project-design proposals were displayed in the Smithsonian Castle in DC for public review and comment prior to the final selection of the Freelon/Adjaye/Bond-Smith Group.

In 2008 Marshall Purnell became the first African American president of the American Institute of Architects in the 150-year history of the organization. For the world of American architecture Purnell's election ranged with overtones of the other big national election of Barack Obama. In that same year the American economy was rapidly sliding into the Great Recession. The repercussions were vast. The architecture profession was certainly not immune. Projects were being canceled. Clients, private and public sector, were not honoring fee payment invoices. The pressures associated with holding the firm together were staggering.

Paul Devrouax unexpectedly died of a massive heart attack at his home on March 22, 2010. Marshall Purnell and the three long time senior associates carried on the practice. In 2012 the firm was restructured around the four senior associates Mark Doswell, Danny Williams, Anthony Brown, and Barbara Laurie (1961-2013) as D&P Partners. In 2014 Purnell left Washington, DC for a full-time appointment as Professor of the Practice in the School of Architecture at North Carolina State University. Today Doswell, Williams, and Brown continue the practice as D&P Partners on a scale that has scant resemblance of the Devrouax and Purnell days of a decade ago. The full Devrouax and Purnell architectural firm story is one that must await the surely forthcoming memoir of Marshall Purnell.

The Freelon Group, Raleigh-Durham, North Carolina

7.18 Phil Freelon, ca 2005.

7.19 Zena Howard, ca 2010. Sources: Wikipedia Commons

North Carolina's Harvey Gantt was not the only young upstart African American architect–practitioner in that state. But it was Gantt whom Travis profiled in his 1991 book. The Freelon Group was only a year old at that point and perhaps understandably was not on the Travis radar. No one could have predicted the Freelon firm's meteoric rise over the next twenty-five years.

Founding partner Phil Freelon (1953-2019) hit the ground running with the opening of his firm's doors in 1990. The firm's clientele list was built from historically black universities and a few politically liberal municipal governments that were eager to give business to a young, obviously talented, technically competent black-owned firm. Architect Zena Howard was Freelon's second in command at the Freelon Group and an indispensable element in helping Freelon grow and manage the firm between 2005 and 2014.

In 2000, I was head of Morgan State University's still fledgling architecture school in Baltimore. That city's planned Maryland Museum of African American History & Culture was stalled in the design stage. I was a member of a city design review panel that rejected the designs proposed by the "salt and pepper" firm initially selected in 1998. Several members of our review panel were asked to help find a replacement firm. After much debate and deliberation, a joint venture between Freelon's firm and Baltimore's RTKL was selected by the Baltimore Museum Committee. Shortly after that, our city review panel joined forces with a state design review panel, which selected the new Freelon–RTKL redesign with great enthusiasm. The completed building's design is as powerful as was promised in the presentation to the joint design review panel.

In 2007, Freelon joined forces with Max Bond to begin pursuing the National Museum of African American History and Culture. British-Ghanaian, London-based David Adjaye was added to the design team along with Smith Group. That team was selected, and the rest, as they say, is history. (see "Introduction," for more on Freelon and the NMAAHC project).

Over the course of his twenty-four year period, between 1990 and 2014, of heading the Freelon Group, Freelon designed dozens of buildings ranging from museums and civil-cultural projects to HBCU campus structures. All of his projects quickly became works that were received with high favor in all quarters across the nation. Freelon is the African American architect who was most instrumental in re-establishing the idea that black architects were or could be members of Black America's culture production wing. His executive leadership on the 2016 completed NMAAHC project was the culminating event in the still unfolding ending of the 100-year-old period of what I opined as the cultural estrangement between Black America and African American architects,

As Freelon grew the firm to nearly fifty persons by 2014, there were over twenty-five regional, state, and local American Institute of Architect (AIA) design awards, including AIA North Carolina's Outstanding Firm Award in 2001. Between 2006 and 2007, the Freelon Group was honored with seven AIA North Carolina design awards, an accomplishment never before achieved by one firm in a two-year period.

In March 2014, the Freelon Group announced that the firm was about to be acquired by global architectural design firm Perkins+Will. Freelon would join the P+W board of directors and become managing partner and design director of the firm's Carolina-area offices. Predictably, the Freelon Group's acquisition by a white-owned firm was cause for consternation and confusion in the African American architect community.

This reaction was similar to the one by much of Black America fourteen years earlier when Robert Johnson sold BET to VIACOM for $2.3 billion in cash and VIACOM stock. There was confusion and consternation. My own thoughts about the deal took me back to a version of something I recall having heard years earlier from another revered black media mogul; "An entrepreneur labors to build a great company and then wait for an offer that he can't refuse."

Knowing what I knew about the difficulty of successfully managing an orthodox architectural firm, I understood the reasons underlying Freelon's decision to join the Perkins+Will behemoth. Freelon's decision was not without a comparable precedent. Interestingly, nearly three decades earlier, Max Bond did something strikingly similar. Bond "merged" his then twenty-five person Harlem-based firm, Bond Ryder Architects, with the downtown New York City-based Davis & Brody architectural firm. Davis & Brody was then a Jewish-owned firm of 120 persons. Bond—a committed academic as well as practitioner—had been offered a full professorship and eventually chairperson role in the prestigious Columbia University School of Architecture and Planning. Bond's reasons for accepting an offer to merge his firm with the Davis Brody firm made great sense.

So, just what would prompt the owner of an apparently successful and revered architectural firm with nearly fifty employees to be willingly absorbed by a 1,000-person global powerhouse firm? The answer in this case may have been all about numbers. For architectural firms everything in between ten and one hundred persons is inherently unstable and often unsustainable.

Prior to starting the Freelon Group, Phil Freelon had spent seven years with O'Brien-Atkins, a majority-owned architectural engineering firm based in the rapidly growing North Carolina Research Triangle. The O'Brien-Atkins firm credits Freelon with a role in its growth from thirty persons when he started there in 1982 to 150 persons when he left in 1989. Freelon had firsthand knowledge of the rules of numbers. He knew precisely what was required to grow an architectural business into the large firm terrain of viability.

Freelon was approaching the age of sixty when he began seriously considering an offer for his firm to be purchased by Perkins+Will. There are many reasons behind his decision but his knowledge about his own health and mortality may have had a bearing. His forty-five person architectural firm was sitting right in the middle of a zone of financial nonviability despite all outward appearances. Such firms face the conundrum of being too small to compete effectively with the one hundred plus-person firms, while at the same time being unable to overpower the multitude of less than twenty person firms. All three size types are challenging for the same projects. Financing is not as available to a fifty person architectural firm as might be assumed. Also, such a size business does not offer an acceptable level of return to equity investors.

7.20 Phil Freelon, ca 2016.
Source: Wikipedia Commons

In July of 2019 Freelon died—to the apparent complete shock and sorrow of the American architecture world. Much of that world had come to know and revere him as one of the most consequential architects of his generation, irrespective of race. Freelon lived to see the successful transition of the entire staff of talented Freelon Group professionals he had recruited and developed between 1990 and 2014 into the Perkins+Will organization. Freelon left a body of work completed by his Freelon Group, including the National Museum of African American History & Culture, that will inspire generations.

The Unicorn: Moody/Nolan, Inc., Columbus, Ohio

7.21. Curtis Moody, CEO Moody/Nolan Inc., Columbus, Ohio, ca, 2017.
Source: Moody/Nolan, Inc and Ben French, photographer.

Moody/Nolan, Inc. (MNI) is a multi-disciplinary architectural–engineering firm that fits the classical definition of a unicorn. MNI is real but is also a statistical zero as African American architectural firms go.

The company was started in 1982 by young architect Curtis Moody, who possessed understandably opportunist objectives: to provide services to the black citizens of his city, Columbus, Ohio, on publicly financed projects being constructed in their neighborhoods. The firm has long since transitioned to full mainstream crossover status while continuing to serve major black institution clients, including historically black colleges and universities.

By the end of his first year, Moody's firm was employing nine people. Moody's first big decision that distinguished him from his professional peers was his entering into a name partnership with a professional engineer rather than another architect-peer.

Two years after opening his doors, Moody merged his company with the civil engineering firm of Howard Nolan. This is rarely done by startup architects, black or white. Over the next eight years, Moody/Nolan, Inc. served an eclectic mix of primarily public-sector clients across the greater Columbus metropolitan region and across the state of Ohio.

By 1991, the year Jack Travis published his book *African American Architects in Current Practice*, Moody/Nolan was already an accomplished firm employing twenty-five persons. By that time, the firm had identified a niche clientele in Ohio's colleges and universities.

Moody and Howard Nolan's alma mater, Ohio State University, was at the core of this niche. The firm logically expanded into successfully marketing its ser-

7.22 Howard Nolan.
Source: Moody/Nolan, Inc.

vices to the nation's more than one hundred historically black colleges and universities (HBCUs). A similar successful move was made toward traditionally white colleges and universities outside of the state of Ohio. Architectural-engineering contracts on several university-based athletic facilities were successfully undertaken. From there it was a short step to MNI's becoming a niche player in the regional marketplace of architect-engineer design services for recreation and athletic facilities.

Today, nearly forty years after Moody opened his doors, the firm is routinely showing up in the middle position of the *Engineering News Record*'s annual listing of the nation's top 500 architectural-engineering companies. Similarly, MNI is ranking in the top one-third of the *Architectural Record*'s annual list of the nation's top 300 architectural firms. *ENR* and *AR* are the industry gold standard as far as measuring success based on annual gross fees and number of employees. As a black-owned firm, MNI sits all alone on such listings.

There is no other black-owned firm in the nation that ranks even a close second to MNI. The firm's annual revenues top $60 million. The staff now numbers 180 persons, a majority being non-black. MNI is really not an aberration when compared to other similar measurements and yardsticks concerning businesses in America. The largest black-owned bank in the nation might not even show up on the list of the nation's 500 largest banks. Similar words apply to construction companies. In the field of architecture, matters are further compounded by the very structure of the architecture profession.

The American Institute of Architects (AIA) reports that at the end of 2018 there were an estimated 20,000 architectural firms in the nation. Fully seventy-five percent of those firms number in personnel from one to nine persons. That seventy-five percent earns a combined fifteen percent share of all business receipts. The next tier of firms is fifteen percent of the total. Their personnel numbers between ten and forty-nine people and earn a combined thirty-two percent of total business receipts. The final 6.5 percent is firms with fifty or more people. This group earns fifty-three percent of all business receipts and further breaks down into sub-groupings of 50 to 100 persons, 100 to 600 persons (considered to be large firms), and a small cluster of firms numbering between 600 and 2,500 persons. There are three firms at the very top of this group that each gross over a billion dollars in annual fees.

Needless to say, black-owned firms—the one hundred or so existing today (down from the two hundred or so that existed in 1991)—are virtually all grouped in the one to nine-person category, with a handful in the ten to forty-nine-person category. Here is the issue: the numbers simply do not work economically until a firm hits the escape velocity of one hundred or more employees. At the one

7.23 Jonathan Moody and Curtis Moody, ca 2018.
Source: Moody/Nolan, Inc.

hundred or more employees' number the relationship between the cost of overhead, business development, and technological infrastructure on the one hand, and professional staff reach the equilibrium required for sustained profitability.

Moody was able to navigate through that unstable minefield of greater than ten but fewer than one hundred employees that is so unforgiving to most architectural firms. Through a perfect alignment of good luck, good timing, the right geography, the right structure, and shrewd financing, MNI has managed to thrive.

Moody has carefully groomed his thirty-five year-old son, Jonathan, a licensed and very seasoned architect who received architecture degrees from Cornell, and the UCLA graduate program. Jonathan is currently the Moody Nolan president and anticipated to eventually succeed his father in the firm's CEO seat.

7.24. Bridge Park, a mixed-use development in downtown Dublin, a Columbus, Ohio suburb. Source: Moody/Nolan, Inc.

Moody invested early and heavily in an effective statewide marketing strategy as well as in productivity-increasing technology infrastructure. Along the way, there had to have been breakthroughs in finding friendly sources and means of financing operations and growth. MNI now appears to have the tools and momentum to continue its current growth for another generation.

Today, Moody/Nolan as lead architect has demonstrated its capacity to undertake and successfully complete projects with construction costs that exceed a quarter of a billion dollars. MNI is the full services lead architectural firm for the large Ohio-based Crawford Howing development company on the Bridge Park development (shown below). The project is comprised of over 1,000 housing units, nearly a million square feet of commercial space-retail space, a global brand hotel, and other amenities. MNI is now positioned financially to actually play the role of being the developer, architect, as well as at-risk builder on projects of this magnitude. Despite such capacity, that may or may not be the course of direction to be taken by MNI.

However, it should be very clear to any architect contemplating starting a firm that a Moody Nolan class firm today cannot be replicated without a robust merger/acquisition strategy and access to equity investment capital. Out of today's possibly one hundred black-owned architectural firms in the nation, the closest comparable companies are the half-dozen black-owned engineering firms. The glaring difference is that the black-owned engineering firms do not design buildings. Those firms bill their mostly public-sector clients as project managers and program managers of large civil-infrastructure construction projects.

8. Three Washington, DC Firms as National Bellwethers

By the close of the 1990s, Barry and the old Black Power crowd that began forming in the late 1960s had lost all control or influence over the financial reins of DC government. Republican party control of a formerly friendly Democrat party-controlled Congress immediately began to cut off previously generous annual appropriations to the DC government. The loss of those funds quickly led to the DC government being declared as insolvent, actually bankrupt. A federally mandated control board was installed to run DC. The Home Rule government was on life support. In 1998 the elected DC government would pass on from Barry to the "civic minded-good government" mayors of first Sharon Pratt Kelly, followed by Mayor Anthony Williams. Though African American, Williams appeared at first to be indifferent to the Black Power–black nationalist zeitgeist that Barry was so committed to.

After two years in power, Williams revealed a positively sophisticated attitude toward black power that was not readily apparent during the early months of his administration. Williams also assembled a cadre of young African American planning and management professionals in policy- and decision-making roles. However, their commitments to the continued utilization of African American-owned architectural firms were far less than in the nearly twenty Barry years.

Meanwhile, over the prior twenty-five year period, the several hundred mostly small white-owned architectural firms in the city had also undergone wholesale transformations. The branch offices of large, national, full-service firms began to dominate the annual listing of the city's twenty-five top fee-grossing architectural firms. None of the second-generation Howard University-trained architectural firm owners were able to capitalize on the tidal wave of nearly a million new people and the attendant private and corporately funded commercial, institutional, and residential growth throughout the region over the prior thirty years. One can only conclude that the development of a substantial, conventionally structured, black-owned architectural practice is more an aberration than a normal occurrence within the existing paradigms of professional practices. This condition holds with only minor variations in every other major metropolitan region in the country, regardless of the size of the non-white core central-city population.

Washington, DC at the close of the twentieth century makes clear a number of things about black architectural practices. The million African Americans living in greater metropolitan Washington were projected to grow in numbers by another half million people by the year 2020. And that has mostly happened. Yet clearly the traditional government-client mainstay of the DC metropolitan region's black architects can no longer provide the basis of healthy growth, stability, or financially and professionally rewarding architectural practices. *A fundamentally new model is essential.* An equally fundamentally new approach in architectural education is also required. Both these things are also eminently doable.

Today the architecture school at Howard has been joined by two other accredited programs. The University of the District of Columbia and Morgan State—fifty minutes up the turnpike in Baltimore—are each struggling valiantly with the issue of defining new missions. The explicit mission at Howard during those 1950-1995 years was the training and socialization of people who would become licensed and go on to establish architectural practices. In today's new world that is still do-able but not without the full reaffirmation of the same explicit mission of produc-ing entrepreneurial practitioners. However, it must also be understood that such practices will differ greatly from twentieth century orthodoxy.

The adoption and effective pursuit of such an explicit mission by any of the currently accredited HBCU-based architecture programs is not likely to occur without the pressure that would grow out of the successful creation of new and possibly independent schools. Such new models targeted at (but not limited to) African Americans are required in order to provide the inherently conser-vative HBCU based programs with concrete evidence of the efficacy of a twen-ty-first century entrepreneur-focused curricula.

Washington, DC's two dozen black-owned architectural firms from just three decades ago have been reduced to at best a dozen firms today. Out of that group, three firms currently stand out, each for a different reason. Each of the three firms, despite being currently structured as orthodox "fee for services" business models, hold the prospect being able to transition to new paths.

The Architecture Firm as Designer-Brander

8.1 Michael Marshall. Source: Courtesy of Michael Marshall Design

Michael Marshall is Washington, DC home-grown with modest working-class roots. His attraction to architecture began early. In his own words, he recalls saying, "I like to draw a lot so I will be an architect." While in high school his mother was a night-shift custodian at the American Institute of Architects national headquarters building in downtown DC. He graduated from high school with no conscious plans of becoming the first in his family to receive a college degree.

In 1975 the University of the District of Columbia's predecessor, Washington Technical Institute, was offering a two-year associate degree program in architectural engineering technology. That provided Marshall with entry to the game. On completion in 1977 his palpable talent led to his entering Catholic University's four-year architecture program as a beginning third-year student. Two years later, his grades at Catholic and a great portfolio got him into Yale's master of architecture program. From 1980 to 1984 Marshall studied in studios run by Frank Gehry and British modernist master James Sterling. Marshall prides himself on qualifying during the pre-computer era when hand drawing and draftsmanship skills were the coin of the realm.

Marshall did the requisite stints as a designer in several local firms before getting his license and taking the leap of hanging out his own shingle in 1989. He did mostly modest-size residential projects. His career-making breakthrough came from designing the palatial new 10,900 square foot Rock Creek Park home of Debra Lee, a Black Entertainment Television executive. Lee interviewed Marshall and several other seasoned architects and selected Marshall's firm, Marshall Moya Design (Paola Moya was his partner). Lee's selection of Marshall as her architect is one of the rare incidents of a very wealthy black entertainment and business mogul consciously (or subconsciously) seeking out a talented African American architect to design a signature residence. Lee's act can be viewed as a reprise of Madam C.J. Walker's having sought out New York architect Vertner Tandy to design her Harlem brownstone salon and her upstate Villa Lewaro mansion over one hundred years ago.

Marshall's ability to deliver on Lee's house in spectacular fashion on this project provided him with the bona fides to pursue larger projects from local developers and public-sector clients. Marshall's success as a design architect for a mainline developer on a sizable downtown mixed-use multi-family–commercial–re-

8.2. Lee Residence, Massachusetts Heights, Rock Creek Park, DC., ca. 2006.
Source: Courtesy of Michael Marshall Design

tail project earned him further credibility.

In 2005, the DC government launched a project to bring talented architects from across the nation to the city to redesign its crumbling stock of public schools. Only the very best local architectural talent could compete in this national design competition. Marshall emerged as one of the DC locals who was rated as highly competitive. He was awarded numerous design contracts including Mann Elementary School in an upscale DC neighborhood.

Marshall's really big breakout project was

8.3. Lee Residence interior

8.4 Lee Residence interior 2.
Sources: Courtesy of Michael Marshall Design

8.5. City Vista Mixed-Use Development at 5th & K Streets, NW DC, Torti Gallis, Architect of Record, Michael Marshall, design phase, ca. 2008. Source: Courtesy of Michael Marshall Design

8.6. Mann School addition and modernization, Washington, DC, ca. 2010.
Source: Courtesy of Michael Marshall Design

his 2016 Student Center for the University of the District of Columbia (UDC). At that time, he was still in partnership with Paola Moya. Their firm, Marshall Moya Design was the design architect in conjunction with Cannon Design as Architect of Record.

This 95,000 square foot building sits in the huge unused plaza space directly in front of the now passé brutalist UDC administrative building. The 40-year-

8.7. UDC Student Center, DC, Cannon Design was Architect of Record, ca. 2016.
Sources: Courtesy of Michael Marshall Design

8.8. UDC Student Center interior atrium 4200 Connecticut Ave, DC, ca. 2016.
Sources: Courtesy of Michael Marshall Design

old Bryant & Bryant-designed project was completed in late-1970s. Marshall's student union project is seen by some as a long overdue correction in bringing UDC out to the Connecticut Avenue street frontage. The contrasting designs may represent an apt passing of the baton from the once reigning Bryants, on through to the succeeding Devrouax & Purnell, and on to Marshall as DC's leading African American architect today.

8.9. United Audi Field, soccer stadium in Southeast DC, ca. 2017.
Source: Courtesy of Michael Marshall Design

Marshall has added a punctuation mark to his status with his role as lead de-sign architect for the United Audi Field Soccer Stadium project that opened in Southeast Washington, DC in 2017. Marshall and his firm were the design lead on a team headed by Populous, the former entertainment and sports facilities design studio within the St. Louis, MO.-based architectural firm HOK.

Marshall sits at the head of a shrinking group of African American-owned Washington, DC architectural firms. At the close of 2018, that group numbered less than a dozen firms, down from the twenty-four that existed in 1978. Mar-shall is very conscious of the predicament facing those who have chosen to practice architecture under the prevailing orthodox contractual arrangements. He recently said that "Architects . . . need to gain back our rightful place in the design and construction process—that we handed over to other 'special-ists'—outside of being legally licensed architects." I am unable to determine to what direction Marshall is prepared to take in acting on his observation about the loss of status of architects as he pursues his stated commitment of being viewed as a first-rate design architect.

The Architecture Firm as Urban Housing Design-Production Team

8.10 Sean Pichon.
Source: Courtesy of PGN Architects

Sean Pichon is a principal in PGN Architects, an interracially owned partnership located in the Capitol Hill section of Washington, DC. Pinchon, a 1995 Howard University graduate, spent his post-school years as a designer in the DC office of international powerhouse Skidmore Owings & Merrill, and later Devrouax and Purnell. His now 16-year old firm of just under 30 people has fashioned a strong niche position inside of DC's largely white-owned group of for-profit multifamily housing developers.,

The firm's early breakout design project was the transformation of a nondescript warehouse into a large office building for local government offices and non-profit community development organizations. The existing structure was expanded to 150,000 square feet and completed in 2003.

8.11 2235 Shannon Place, Southeast Washington, DC. Source: Courtesy of PGN Architects

8.12. The Elysium 14th Street, a luxury condo in the U Street area ca 2018.
Source: Courtesy of PGN Architects

8.13. 1530 1st Street, SW, 101 affordable units. Southwest DC.
Source: Courtesy of PGN Architects

8.14. 600 T Street, NW, 79 luxury units, NW DC. Source: Courtesy of PGN Architects

This was the kind of project delivery by a young firm that turns heads. Since then, PGN has clearly made a commitment to focusing on high-density multifamily housing. Becoming a trusted, go-to firm to a cross-section of local, majority-owned developers requires a very deliberate and strategic effort. The firm's client list ranges from major non-profit community developers to several frontline for-profit developers. Direct contracts from DC government agencies do not appear to be a factor in the firm's workload. The firm knows the games of zoning and development finance better than its very knowledgeable clients.

Those clients operate under a business model that entails buying expensive land and extracting every square foot of zoning entitlements. PGN also clearly understands the imperatives of deploying state of the art computer tools for project design.

The possibility that Pichon's PGN business model can be scaled up to a zone of sustainable financial viability exists. A possible orthodox model is Handel Architects, a now twenty-five-year-old New York City-based white-owned firm. I cite Handel Architects because that is the firm recently hired by the nation's three largest black developers whose three-way consortium was recently selected to develop, build and market a $1.2 billion mixed use (with mainly residential units) skyscraper in Los Angeles.

Handel Architects founding partner Gary Handel started the firm in 1994 when he was 45 years old. To start a firm from scratch and in twenty-five years grow to nearly 200 staff architects that have designed nearly 40,000 housing units in mostly mid- and high-rise buildings is not something that just happens.

8.15. 303-unit Valvaere Apartments on Benning Road, SE DC. Source: Courtesy of PGN Architects

Handel was a mid-career architect working at a high level in the office of KPF, one of the nation's most prestigious corporate architecture firms. Handel's meteoric rise is rooted in deliberate strategy he deployed in starting his firm. He did not start his new firm by chasing random projects. He started with a solid contractual commitment from at least one very large developer client he had cultivated during his former days as an employee That client was seeking the certainty of delivery from Handel. Once Handel delivered, he merely needed to replicate his successes with other like-minded developers he had formerly worked with. Handel's laser-like focus on high density urban housing made his firm a preferred choice for real estate developers.

Given the projected growth of the greater Washington, DC national capital region there could be a half-dozen highly focused "Handel-type" one hundred person architectural firms that laser-focus on residential design. However, the growing impact of artificial intelligence and algorithmic design tools pose an existential threat to even the Handel Architects over the next two decades or less.

A plausible strategy today for a small but highly focused firm like PGN that is seeking to reach financial viability and sustainability would be to pursue other alternative hybrid business models. A merger or acquisition of PGN by a well-capitalized real estate developer or contractor—or better yet, both—would be a happy growth opportunity. That hybrid new business model is also replicable. The alternative of stasis will result in an outcome that is preordained.

The Architecture Firm as Multifaceted Profit Centers (Through A Merger and Acquisitions Strategy)

8.16 Kathy Dixon, ca 2016.
Source: Courtesy of Kathy Dixon Architecture.

Kathy Dixon, a recent inductee to the AIA College of Fellows, is a 1991 Howard University architecture graduate who also holds a master's in city planning from UCLA. Dixon spent two decades working at senior levels in several highly reputable Washington, DC–based architecture and engineering firms before going out on her own in 2011. Dixon recently completed a two-year term as the third female to be elected president in the nearly fifty-year history of the National Organization of Minority Architects. She is a senior professor in the University of the District of Columbia's architecture school.

Dixon—in one of the rare instances of an architect actually writing a book—released *The Business of Architecture: Your Guide to a Financially Successful Firm* (2018, Routledge). This is a fresh, quick, must-read that should be required in the first year of any professional-degree architecture program. Dixon's blunt words and dire warnings about the existential state of the practice of architecture in today's world can seem overwrought on first reading. The reality is that she may be understating the prospects of extinction and irrelevance for all but the handful of today's mega-size practices. Her allusions to the near future containing only mega firms that employ over one thousand persons (unless more sound business practices are adopted) are convincing.

In Dixon's book she succinctly lays out the rules that any successful business must obey and then provides concrete examples of how architects must apply those rules to their architectural practices. She goes where architecture faculties and academic cultures forbid: the issue of money and the need for architecture practices to make not just a little but *lots of money*. She is simply pointing out that for-profit businesses must be organized to be actually *profitable*. She injects reasoned concepts about why orthodox architecture culture's "do not expect to make money" dictum is a fatal flaw.

Whether intended or not Dixon is championing the business model of a well-known mega-size practice known simply as AECOM. Three decades ago, AECOM began expanding beyond its base as a large one hundred plus person architectural engineering firm to that of a gigantic and globally far-flung conglomerate of acquired companies. Each company engages in some aspect of the making of the physical environment. The AECOM companies are called "profit centers." There are AECOM companies that actually construct a wide variety of building types. Others construct infrastructure projects that range from rapid transit systems to utilities systems. There are also AECOM companies that are real estate development entities. AECOM capitalization is acquired through the company's listing on the New York Stock Exchange. Moody/Nolan Inc, the nation's largest black-owned architect-engineer firm could be considered as a possible miniature version of AECOM.

In 2016, Dixon engaged in practicing what she preaches. She provided a very concrete example of what she wrote in her book. She took the first step on the road to the "mergers and acquisitions" business strategy for taking her small boutique firm to the next level. She had the foresight to acquire a controlling interest in a 70-year-old, well-regarded, white-owned architectural firm. She is now the CEO of a firm that is substantially larger than her old firm was. She now has a mid-Atlantic region client base, a larger staff, and a broader range of services to offer.

After providing her readers with a clear description of business structure options, business models, profit centers, and communications strategies, it was inevitable that she would include a clearly written chapter titled "The Architect as the Developer." Dixon delegated the writing of this chapter to her business partner, Karl L. Moody, a graduate architect who operates as a corporate entrepreneur. Moody reminds architects that they are in the real estate business and are superbly positioned to combine that reality with their building design skills. Moody provides concrete examples in making a convincing case that being a competent, design-sensitive architect *and* a real estate developer is the only viable option for all but a small group of the current and coming generation of American architects. Moody provides examples of firms that have been successfully using that business model over the past several decades. Clearly, this modus operandi is going to grow. The risks are more than offset by the increased financial rewards and capacity to control project outcomes.

Dixon, as a strong advocate for achieving growth and transformation through a mergers and acquisition strategy, makes a solid case for architects to lead with a "big picture" orientation. The organizational structure of her firm demonstrates her keen grasp of the issues that must be confronted by all design professionals. Currently, her firm is well positioned to transition to a twenty-first-century business model that also aligns with the ideas, tools, and techniques she has provided in her thoughtful book.

While each of the previous three Washington, DC architect-practitioners may be able to grow and transition their firms into a viable hybrid business model, none have made a convincing case that this will happen. Each must find a pathway to either of several alternative business models that are required in a future that has already arrived. The outlines of such viable alternative models can best be gleaned from a cursory look at two representative companies. Both of the companies, profiled briefly in chapter ten, can be argued as being a (projected) twenty-first century version of an architecture practice that is separate from the "designer and story-telling" architectural firms that have dominated the architectural press.

If such companies are not formed by licensed black architects, acting in concert or partnerships with other disciplines, the current trend of rapidly disappearing African American-owned architectural firms will only accelerate. Variations of new practices, modeled on the chapter ten companies, are the only conceivable route to meaningful participation in meeting the housing and community development needs of the forty-four million-strong group we know today as Black America.

PART III
ARCHITECTS AND BLACK AMERICA 2020–2030

**Realigning
Architecture
with the Black Agenda**

---

9. Black America Must Build Something!
... One Million New Housing Units By 2030

> "Architecture does not come from design…
> architecture comes from capital [money]"

Those were words spoken fifty years ago by a Harvard Graduate School of Design classmate of mine who came to this country from his Scandinavian country homeland. Back then I thought that his words were perhaps astute but overly abstract and simplistic.

Architects today are confronted with this reality; every single set of drawings, videos, and photographs of the buildings and other artifacts that make up the man-built environment now in existence on earth have now been captured as digitized random access memory, linkable to artificial intelligence-derived algorithms, and computer-deliverable as "virtual reality." We can now produce simulated new environments that are measurable, repeatable, and predictable in all critical respects before anything is ever actually built. All of that digitized memory (and money) now moves around the globe at the speed of light. Everything is happening at an exponentially accelerating rate of change.

The next wave of African American architects must now learn how to use the combination of available, off the shelf twenty-first century information technology and capital (money) to develop, design, and build houses, blocks, neighborhoods, communities, and even new cities. That group of architects must begin by resisting the intuitive urge of seeking guidance from other mainstream orthodox architects and architecture-centered manifestos.

9.1 Marc Morial. Source: Wikipedia Commons

They must instead do several other things not normally done by formally trained architects. The very first thing is to carefully read the last several National Urban League Annual State of Black America Reports, prepared under the guiding hand of executive director Mark Morial, a former two-term mayor of New Orleans. The Urban League reports paint a grim picture about the economic and financial well-being of Black America as a *group* among America's competing groups.

The Reports portray Black America as an entity with a population of over forty million people and an annual GDP that would rank sixteenth on the list of the world's 195 nations. Black America is a vast consumer market and political bloc that is represented by the Congressional Black Caucus.

Each one of today's forty plus million people who check U.S. census boxes as "black" or African American are not merely the descendants of persons who were slaves in America over a period that lasted 250 years. They are the descendants of the people whose labor, pain and suffering provided the wealth that literally built America. They are the people who despite a succeeding 100 years of unspeakably cruel oppression after slavery, gave the nation its culture, its soul, its conscience, and its status as an actual democracy with the enactments of the 1964-65 Civil Rights and Voting Rights acts.

Some things are strongly implied in the Urban League annual reports, though never explicitly stated. One of those implied things is for Black America's leadership to advocate that Black America must *"BUILD* SOMETHING!" ... *something that is really big, really sustainable, really scalable, really financially plausible, and that is sure to accelerate the creation of black wealth.*

Today, African American architects are positioned to directly respond to the clearly implied *"BUILD* SOMETHING!" exhortation. Such a response could elevate black architects to a level of essentiality in Black America as has always been intuitively seen with medical doctors and lawyers. A sizable group of African American architects must seize the time by initiating just such a movement for a focused group enterprise project to:

"Build One Million Affordable Houses Over the Next Ten Years."

Such a movement would quickly generate the second thing that a break away wing of African American architects must do: identify the tools and resources required to implement such a big idea aimed at radically altering the status quo in Black America. Many of those tools and resources are hidden in plain sight in places that are also not where architects are inclined to look.

> The American Housing and Economic Mobility Act [AHEMA] takes a comprehensive approach to the housing crisis, tackling affordable housing supply through a $450 billion investment over a decade into the Housing Trust Fund . . . and closes the racial wealth gap by providing down payments to first-time homebuyers in formerly redlined neighborhoods or segregated areas.
>
> –Sen. Elizabeth Warren (D-MA)

9.2. Congresswoman Gwen Moore (D-WI), Senator Elizabeth Warren (D-MA), and Congressman Cedric Richmond (D-LA), in press conference introducing new housing legislature, ca. 2018. Source: Wikipedia Commons

The AHEMA is a newly enacted legislative initiative that could provide the Black America described by Morial and the National Urban League with the tools to fashion a thus far conspicuously missing networked African American dominated multi-billion-dollar national housing industry. There is also the Green New Deal, an idea that erupted from the 2018 midterm elections and is now a congressional resolution. Then there is the Opportunities Zone Act. The OZA is now legislation that provides a physical place framework for all of the other initiatives under a progressive oriented government. The OZA—progressively modified—may be the most relevant piece of legislation of all.

A casual click and scroll through a U.S. map showing all of the designated opportunity zones (**www.opportunitydb.com/tools/map/**) is illuminating. One will find highlighted census tracts that are a blaring green light to the trillions of dollars of under-invested private capital in the U.S. The land areas could easily accommodate added population numbers that would exceed the current U.S. urban population.

In addition to all of these legislative initiatives we must remind ourselves that the current U.S. tax code has created an existing robust affordable-housing industry. That industry has produced millions of new housing units since the tax code law enactment in 1987. Only a miniscule portion of the hundreds of billions of dollars expended in development, design, construction, and management costs have accrued to Black America's people, businesses, and key institutions. In most instances, black business inclusion in that multi-billion-dollar industry is conspicuously small and incidental—actually measuring in at a statistical zero percentage amount.

The industry, as currently constituted, is comprised of two lists maintained by AFFORDABLE HOUSING FINANCE MAGAZINE (a Hanley-Wood Publication).

The lists are The *Affordable Housing 50 Owners* and *The Affordable Housing Developers*. The availability of new legislative tools offers tremendous opportunities for dramatically increasing the black presence in the now three decades old tax code-fueled affordable housing industry.

This is a set of companies that specialize in the annual collective building of tens of thousands of affordable-housing units mostly in cities and near suburbs. These companies do this using a combination of public and private funds in a formulaic way. The industry as presently constituted is actually a helter-skelter collection of pre-information age operations.

However, the industry now faces grave threats from arising new enterprises fueled by massive amounts of investment capital seeking to disrupt the construction industry. Those new companies are seeking market share in the consensus agreed upon U.S. shortage of 7.3 million affordable houses. These upstart companies seek to bring lower costs to the building of affordable housing through full integration of the silos of capital, design, and construction.

A dedicated, motivated, appropriately organized, and properly educated segment of the next generation of African American architects—hopefully abetted by HBCUs—must emulate the disrupters. Doing so requires determined, deliberate, focused, and immediate movement in Black America's drive towards a dominant position in the affordable housing industry. An apostate wing of architects that re-invent itself to literally build one million–plus housing units over the next decade will also acquire the capability to build the second million houses over a following five-year period.

"Make No Little Plans...They Fail to Stir the Hearts of Men..."

-Daniel Burnham, Executive Architect
Chicago World's Fair ca 1890

As the larger America prepares to embark upon a long overdue multiyear multi-trillion-dollar infrastructure rebuilding program, black architect-practitioners—the ones who chose to join the National Urban League in championing the economic interest of Black America—would be in the forefront of the launch of a moon shot. That thrust could dramatically accelerate the national conversation now starting to take place about how to actually close the chronic gaps behind other American groups as depicted in the Urban League State of Black America Report(s).

Today's corps of African American architects must immediately acquire a clear-eyed understanding of what has *really* been happening in much of Black America's physical spaces between Dr. King's April 4, 1968 assassination and today.

That fifty-year period saw massive rebuilding in central-city communities across the nation. There were hundreds of billions of dollars in public and private sector funds expended. With some irony, those billions of spent dollars can now be seen as having abetted a failed Marshall Plan that had been called for in the 1960s by the National Urban League. Despite undeniable gains and progress for many individuals, the 1970s era start of inner-city redevelopment has left African Americans as a group (Black America) worse off.

The list of the redevelopment initiatives were seemingly endless. There was The

War on Poverty, The Great Society, The Equal Opportunity Act, Model Cities, Affirmative Action, Black Capitalism, The Community Development Act, and so on, ad nauseum. All of this was done in the name of "rebuilding" mostly urban neighborhoods in cities that began exploding in violence in 1964. The stream of redevelopment initiatives even included a federally funded exurban New Towns Act as part of President Lyndon B. Johnson's War on Poverty and Great Society.

The early 1980s period of urban inner-city rebuilding coincided with the rise of a new architect-led movement called *New Urbanism (NU)*. That movement illustrates the importance of a big idea that elevated community- and city-building over the design of object single buildings. The New Urbanism movement's tactics and strategies holds valuable lessons for twenty-first century African American architects determined to make a lasting positive impact on the plight of Black America.

New Urbanism actually began as an exurban and small towns idea. The movement was largely founded by politically savvy and socially conscious west coast university faculty-based architect-planner-practitioners. Those architects were quickly joined by like-minded Atlantic Coast cohorts. New Urbanism never carried a hint of racism or hostility to African American interests. Yet for a host of reasons New Urbanism was a mainly all-white affair. By 1993, New Urbanism had a charter. The following paragraph captures the tone, tenor, and policy aims of the movement:

> We advocate the restructuring of public policy and development practices to support the following principles: neighborhoods should be diverse in use and population; communities should be designed for the pedestrian and transit as well as the car; cities and towns should be shaped by physically defined and universally accessible public spaces and community institutions; urban places should be framed by architecture and landscape design that celebrate local history, climate, ecology, and building practices.

New Urbanism was considered by many thoughtful planning and design professionals to be the first really new movement in architectural design and planning since the then sixty-year-old modernist movement began in earnest earlier in 1940s America. The NU claims of being a radical new movement was historically accurate despite biting criticisms of its being intellectually pretentious, elitist, and superficial. The lengthy charter served as proof that the NU founders and followers, calling themselves the Congress of New Urbanism (CNU), was indeed a serious *movement*. The NU founders heeded some of the most socially progressive thinking that preceded the movement. Jane Jacobs, author of the influential 1961 book *The Death and Life of Great American Cities*, was the American spiritual godmother of the NU movement.

The New Urbanism capture of inner city and public housing design and planning leadership was perhaps inevitable. Hundreds of new community redevelopment projects sprung up across the nation, most in big cities, and many on the sites of large, black and brown populated housing projects. By the late

1980s the movement had literally captured the US Department of Housing and Urban Development (HUD) as a key source of seed funding and intellectual legitimacy. HUD adopted the CNU charter and made it official public policy.

NU theories, and its architect–planner consultants, were fully adopted by the nation's most savvy and aggressive urban developers and local public policy officials. HUD made the incorporation of NU design and planning principles conditions for funding projects.

By 2004, New Urbanism was in full swing under the new HUD initiative known as HOPE VI (Housing Opportunities for People Everywhere). This new HUD program began in 1992 and saw nearly $6 billion of public funds being poured into the remake of "the projects." The nation's largest, most troubled (and almost always occupied totally by black or brown people) public-housing sites became prime objects for being leveled by dynamite and rebuilt at doubled, tripled, sometimes larger numbers of mostly upscale and expensive housing units on the same plot of ground. The dynamiting actually started in 1972 at the Pruitt Igo projects in St. Louis, MO. Upon its initial construction completion this project was showered with accolades and design awards by the architecture profession. The photograph of the destruction of Pruitt Igo is a globally iconic symbol of the failures in American social housing design in pre-New Urbanism modern architecture.

The HOPE VI program would for many prove to be a reincarnation of the 1960s era of leveling communities, neighborhoods, and houses occupied by large swaths of Black America. Back then this was carried out under the banner of Urban Renewal, an initiative that eventually became known across Black America as Negro Removal.

In all cases the rebuilding preconstruction funding for the re-design and re-development of the Pruitt Igo's of America came from HUD. There was a torrent of money in the form of grants, low-interest loans, loan guarantees, and tax credits for developers. Needless to say, those developers (and their architects and con-

9.3 Pruitt Igo public housing project demolition, St. Louis, MO., ca 1972.
Source: Wikipedia Commons

struction contractors) were rarely black or other underrepresented minorities.

The NU founding architects, along with additional, strategically located white-owned architecture and planning firms, remade their practices to serve the needs of very savvy and virtually all-white developers. Black planning and design firms were rarely selected for inclusion on the redesign and rebuilding of the failed inner-city public-housing projects across Black America. Washington, DC and Baltimore, MD were exceptions to this rule though only to limited degrees.

Here is part of the mission statement of one of the dominant architectural firms that spent its first thirty years between 1953 and 1983 as a prolific designer of mostly white suburban tract houses and garden-style apartment communities throughout Washington, DC. Keep in mind that these are words from an *architectural firm* rather than a developer or planning firm:

> We understand that developer-driven real estate production is one of the entities that give form to the city. And we recognize the power of the ordinary dwelling. Absent a sense of place, however, its impact is very limited. Our goal is to elevate the quality of everyday environments, bringing dignity to housing and more power to the places they make. Our work is about making the background buildings that line the city's ordinary streets and squares, in which daily life unfolds. Simply put, we are the designers of the fabric of the city and strive to make the most beautiful things out of the simplest clay.

> —Torti Gallis+ Partners, *Architects of Community*, 2016

The public housing project and surrounding community where I grew up in the Watts section of Los Angeles was filled with mostly black and brown people and has been undergoing redevelopment over the past thirty years. Virtually all of the redevelopment work is being done by a dedicated movement comprised of developers, builders, suppliers, design and engineering professionals, skilled workers, and others who rarely and only incidentally look like me or the people living in these places. Changing that dynamic requires a counter-movement that is just as professionally competent and driven as the New Urbanists and their developer clients.

African American-owned architectural firms as we have known them simply cannot provide a meaningful impact on the big issues facing Black America without a similar New Urbanist-type movement. Such a movement has to be about something far bigger than the grievances of architects who persist in adhering to the orthodox dogma of established architecture culture.

While black architects can fully ascribe to many of the New Urbanism planning and design principles, there are fundamental differences. I liken those differences to the ones that distinguish a Historically Black College or University from a Historically White College or University; many of the same textbooks, especially in the hard sciences…but vastly differing objectives and outcomes relative to the health, welfare, and well-being of the inhabitants of Black America. The following words are excerpts from a lengthy paper on urban housing in the 2017 National Urban League State of Black America Report. The words are those of Dr. Ron Daniels, President of the Institute of the Black World.

9.4 Ron Daniels, ca. 2017. Source: Institute of the Black World/Wikipedia Commons

> "Gentrification has emerged as a major threat to Black communities that have been centers of Black political, civic, business, economic and cultural development for generations. Gentrification has become a watchword signaling the displacement of Black people and Black culture. In short, gentrification is the "Negro Removal Program" of the twenty-first century…. Cities are generally hubs of metropolitan political and economic power…"

Daniels continues;

> "Can strategies be devised that prioritize improving the lives of current residents while preserving the culture and character of their communities? The answer to both questions is yes. The collective brainpower, skill, experience and will exist within Black America to defend Black communities against gentrification. We not only possess this collective genius; we must deploy it or be displaced."

Revisiting Big (African American) Ideas Since 1966

On Black America's need to "BUILD SOMETHING…spectacularly big," we need to revisit and retrace three key examples of big ideas that began during the 1960s. The first two examples, Soul City, North Carolina and Fort Lincoln New Town in Washington, DC, were both born inside of President Lyndon Johnson's Great Society-War on Poverty movement. The third example, Buy the Block, surfaced in 2013. The revisiting of big valid ideas and concepts today could be the key to collective action that could lead directly to the substantial increases of Black America's perennially low levels of ownership and wealth.

Soul City, North Carolina

Lee Bey, a Chicago based writer and photographer, is possibly the only one in America who looks like him that is actually recognized in the mainstream press as an "architecture critic." Bey, writing in a 2016 article in the *Guardian*, raised the timely question of why Floyd McKissick's valiant struggle to develop the new town of Soul City failed. Bey's observations track closely with my own.

9.5 Lee Bey.
Source: Wikipedia Commons

9.6. Martin Luther King, Floyd McKissick, and Stokely Carmichael, Mississippi ca 1966. Source: Wikipedia Commons

McKissick left as head of the Congress of Racial Equality (CORE) in 1968 to pursue his vision of literally building a new town in Warren County, North Carolina. Soul City was one of fourteen new towns proposed by an American president. Soul City was envisioned by McKissick as having a population of 55,000 people on a 5,000-acre tract of land.

"A fresh start" was the slogan coined by McKissick who was ideologically positioned squarely between Dr. Martin Luther King's dreams of racial integration and Stokely Carmichael's dream of Black Power.

McKissick insisted that Soul City would be open to all races. He was equally committed to the proposition that Soul City's distinction would be that African Americans would be the main planners, designers, builders, and owners of most of the city's land and business enterprises.

9.7 Harvey Gantt. Source: Wikipedia Commons

9.8 James Rouse.
Source: Time Magazine cover August 1981/Wikipedia Commons

McKissick enlisted the aid of young black North Carolina architect Harvey Gantt, a recent recipient of an MIT graduate planning degree. Gantt had earlier experienced nationally televised images of his bitterly contested racial integration of the Clemson University architecture program in South Carolina. McKissick also hired the prominent New York City-based black-owned architectural firm, Ifill and Johnson (see page 76).

9.9 Columbia, MD model of the town center of the planned city, ca 1968.
Source: Wikipedia Commons

9.10 Soul City, Warren County North Carolina, ca 2016. Source: Wikipedia Commons

Soul City's founder and his planners had what they considered to be the perfect model in the planned new town of Columbia, Maryland. Columbia's visionary founder, James Rouse, geographically positioned Columbia midway between Baltimore, MD and Washington, DC. Rouse and his planners envisioned a town of 110,000 people of all races living in social harmony in the 14,000-acre development.

Columbia met and surpassed all of its target goals. Today an aerial view of the Town Center and city beyond looks largely identical to the 1968 architectural model of the proposed city. Today's Columbia is a city of 100,000 people whose population is roughly 50% white and 50% non-white with African Americans making up half of the non-white population. Rouse went on to become a legend in the world of planned urban development.

For Soul City, McKissick managed to scrape together a few million dollars in federal money for infrastructure costs. McKissick was unable to overcome huge obstacles, such as the 1974 Mideast oil crisis, the Watergate scandal distractions, and the racial politics of arch-conservative North Carolina U.S. senator Jesse Helms. Nor was McKissick able to attract the necessary private investment capital and debt financing commensurate with the money raised by Rouse for Columbia. Soul City's population never exceeded two hundred people.

Today, nearly fifty years after Floyd McKissick was forced to fold on his dream of building a successful Soul City in North Carolina there are tools, conditions, and attitudes in place that scream "try this again!" There are possibly as many as one hundred geographic locations in the U.S. that mirror the conditions that made Columbia a socio-economic, cultural and financial success. Timing, location, and branding are still all-important.

Whether a group of African Americans can aspire to build new cities of 100,000 people—with highly probable majority black populations—and not be assumed to be black separatists is a huge question mark. That question must be addressed head on by action. The Columbia, MD new town experiment was a success and can be replicated today in similar locations that are in proximity to one or more U.S. cities.

Fort Lincoln New Town, Washington, DC

The 1960s era vision of a "New Town in Town" in Washington, DC was implemented by Theodore Hagans, Jr. (1925-1984). Hagans was an engineering degree holder from the Howard University School of Engineering and Architecture. Before embarking on building Fort Lincoln, Hagans had achieved success as a real estate developer and rental property owner. Fort Lincoln New Town was born in the same time span as Columbia in Maryland and Soul City in North Carolina. The reasons for Fort Lincoln New Town were largely similar to the ones behind Columbia and Soul City: President Johnson wanted a model example of what could happen through his War on Poverty-Great Society programs. In this case the site chosen was a nearly 360-acre parcel of vacant land siting on the DC border of Prince Georges County, Maryland but still just several short miles from downtown DC and the national capitol building.

9.11 Fort Lincoln New Town master plan, Northeast Washington, DC ca 1995.
Source: Wikipedia Commons

This too was a very big idea that involved bold initiative of a coalition of progressive politics and black development entrepreneurial vision. By the mid-1970s, Hagans—a former classmate of the Bryant & Bryant architectural firm heads, Charles and Robert—was becoming the largest black developer in DC. Hagans became the sole owner of all rights to redevelop Fort Lincoln New Town, a 362-acre planned community located on the northeastern border of DC. The project master plan called for thousands of new homes and apartment buildings, with a shopping mall, public schools, and recreational facilities.

Hagans originally started out at Fort Lincoln as the "minority" partner. The lead white developer had assembled nine all-white architectural firms (out of a total of ten) to do all of the planning and design for the project. That developer eventually tired of the political hassle he was getting from the mostly black middle- and lower-middle-class community immediately adjacent to the site. The project fell to Hagans, who immediately severed all existing contractual relations with the white architectural firms. Under Hagans, seven of DC's black-owned firms (mostly all owned by Howard University graduates) and one Asian American firm received new contracts. The largest contract, including the role of executive architect for master planning, went to Bryant & Bryant. This was another example of the fraternal political ties between the Bryants and DC's black power brokers who could directly or indirectly select architects to receive design contracts.

It has taken fifty years to reach the halfway mark of full achievement of the Fort Lincoln New Town vision. The project is being completed under the ownership and executive leadership of his daughter Michelle Hagans who is also a Howard engineering graduate. Conditions and circumstances today are ripe for the replication of the Hagans family's Fort Lincoln New Town vision in at least fifty other U.S. cities over the coming decades.

Buy the Block

The third and quite possibly most important big idea is a five-year-old movement that is already gaining momentum throughout Black America's urban-suburban population. This movement's participants range from the black new rich to the black poor. The movement is simply known as "Buy the Block."

Buy the Block was founded by Lynn P. Smith in Cincinnati in 2013. Smith has been a serial entrepreneur and real estate investor since she turned twenty-one. From the 2013 founding of BTB Smith has created investment vehicles that are catalyzing precisely the actions that are continuing to happen across Black America at a geometrically accelerating pace. Her idea is scalable from the single house or lot in an urban neighborhood and on up to the creation of a new urban city.

I have spent my entire professional life inside of the world of orthodox architecture culture at its most elitist level, whether in the white part (the American Institute of Architects), or the black part (the National Organization of Minority Architects). Predictably, when thinking about alternative and counter models one is intuitively drawn to other elitist models. After considerable thinking it finally dawned on me that there already was a *movement* that was as fittingly large, clear, and compelling as the 1980s architect-led New Urbanism movement.

The "Buy the Block" name is profoundly elegant, succinct, and inclusive of all of the socio-economic class stratifications in Black America. The BTB movement totally captures the spirit and the need of a counter movement. The twenty-first

9.12 Lynn P. Smith, founder of Buy the Block ca 2016. Source: Amy Cortese. September 2018

century generation of architects as community and city builders may have in BTB the ideal model for carrying out the goal of building one million housing units over the next decade.

Nothing comes close to the Buy the Block movement as the vehicle and set of organizing and philosophical principles. A Buy the Block thrust is already an integrated amalgam of elements and membership from a number of other groups. No one is excluded on the basis of their race, ethnicity, or religion. That would be in the same vein as a typical historically black college or university (HBCU) or the National Organization of Minority Architects (NOMA).

However, like those organizations, the measurable priority of people and interests served would be those of Black America. Accordingly, expanding and upgrading Black America's institutional deficits would be a priority. Given the base skill set of the new movement, the absence of a robust housing industry able to produce housing for Black America's market population would be an obvious first target to be attacked.

This grassroots movement is, intentionally or not, providing the prospect of making *architecture* as essential in Black America as is medicine and law. All that is necessary is for architects to grasp the genius logic of Buy the Block and follow things to the logical conclusion. It is Buy the Block concepts that are going to move the needle upward on Black America's big metric deficits of home ownership and family wealth ratios, and the creation of viable business and economic development.

Resources and Capital in Black America

There is currently no shortage of opinions, plans, and proposals for what must be done to bring economic parity to Black America. Many of those plans have merit, some more than others. In some way, all of those plans are necessary. Still missing from all of those plans is one that promotes a group effort by the Black America that has been so compellingly portrayed by the National Urban League year after year in the Annual State of Black America Report.

The totally disruptive information technology forces that were unleashed fifty years ago have also created a new mogul-class of black entrepreneurs in the music, film, TV, finance, computer, and real estate industries. Some of these entrepreneurs arrived at mogul status from careers in major league athletic endeavors. Many of these men and women are coming around to the view that using their own wealth, know-how, and access to capital to improve Black America is the right thing for them to do. Many are just now arriving at that mindset but a significant number of others have been doing their part for many years.

This awakening of a black moneyed class to their responsibilities (and also major opportunities) bodes well for the future of an eventually economically healthy Black America. This new class is more than willing to open doors for other blacks. However, what they cannot and will not do is ignore or disobey the physics of investment capital. Black real estate developers will rarely represent a source of work for orthodox black architectural firms. The exception might be the outlier 180-person Moody/Nolan firm based in Columbus, Ohio.

A number of the new money class of African Americans have made their fortunes by convincing traditionally white-controlled (and Asian) sources of vast institutional funds to entrust them with money to develop the real estate in traditionally black communities. A small group of African American real estate developers began enticing and successfully using white institutional money in the 1980s. Several of those developers have been able to open doors for younger black real estate developers within the last two decades.

9.13 A.R. Bernard.
Source: Wikipedia Commons

A high-profile big idea is the $1.2 billion project now in the advanced planning stage in Brooklyn, New York. The project is being spearheaded by pastor A.R. Bernard. His 40,000-member megachurch, Christian Cultural Center, is developing a large tract of land next door to the church complex that will accommodate 2,000 new affordable-housing units. Pastor Bernard is a former member of the Nation of Islam and is undoubtedly committed to black economic development.

9.14 Quinton Primo, III.
Source: Wikipedia Commons

9.15 Roland Wiley.
Source: Courtesy of RAW International

9.16 3D rendering of the master plan of the Baldwin Hills Crenshaw Plaza expansion. Source: Courtesy of RAW International

However, he is working in partnership with a large, established, majority-owned New York City development company. Typically, such a company comes with its own long-established commitments and relationships with majority architects, contractors, suppliers, and labor groups. Pastor Bernard is highly representative of scores of the nation's black megachurches in their quests to develop affordable housing on or near their church properties. However good their intentions, more often than not, they are compromised on the issue of maximizing dollar flow into African American hands and businesses.

The Baldwin Hills Crenshaw Plaza shopping mall in south central Los Angeles has been a symbol of black middle-class affluence as long as I can remember. The complex is located about ten miles from my old neighborhood in the Watts community of South-Central Los Angeles. The 550,000 square feet mall first opened in 1947 when that part of Los Angeles was still an all-white community. By the 1960s the surrounding Baldwin Hills Crenshaw community was beginning to be populated largely by middle- and high-income African Americans.

The mall continues to be a huge symbol of pride to that community. In 2006 the mall was acquired by Chicago-based Capri Capital Partners, an African American owned company founded in 1992 by hedge fund manager Quinton Primo, III. Primo is a 65-year-old real estate developer with an impressive record of accomplishments. Today his company holds $3.7 billion in real estate equity and structured finance investments. In 2012 Black Enterprise Magazine named Capri Capital as its Financial Services Company of the year.

Primo's plan for the 43-acre Baldwin Hills property is to add two million square feet to the now 800,000 square feet mall complex. The additions planned include 1,000 new residential units, a new hotel, added commercial space, and additional parking structures.

Capri retained RAW International to prepare the master plan. RAW is a small Los Angeles-based architecture, urban design, and transportation planning firm. RAW was founded and owned by Roland Wiley, a licensed architect. The extent of participation in actual building design by Wiley's firm and other local black-owned construction companies, suppliers, and other business enterprises is still to be determined.

Another high-profile project initiative by black American developers is the recently announced Angels Landing Development, a $1.2 billion mixed-use project in downtown Los Angeles. The project was awarded to a joint-venture team of three black super developers, Victor MacFarlane of San Francisco, Richard Pagan (black Hispanic) of New York City, and Don Peebles, Jr. of Miami. Today those three men are at or near the top of a list of possibly three-dozen large black developers spread around the nation. Earvin "Magic" Johnson, another household name across Black America, also sits high on this list of black super developers. The projects by the black super developers are not always "black" projects in the sense that the users and occupants will be predominantly black.

The three super developers selected Hamel Architects; a white-owned 200-person firm based in New York City. Hamel is a 25-year-old firm that has designed hundreds of residential projects, mostly high-rise apartment buildings totaling more than 40,000 units.

9.17 Angel's Landing, Los Angeles.
Source: Wikipedia Commons

Despite the past pattern of black super developers not utilizing black architectural firms as lead designers on their projects, black super-developer, Don Peebles, Jr., one of the three developers of the Angels landing project, has opened up an extraordinary new avenue of opportunity. Peebles announced his plan to raise a new $500 million fund for use by primarily minority developers.

There are no rules, laws or policies precluding the existing and soon to emerge next corps of licensed African American architects from doing what non-architect real estate development CEOs routinely do. The issue is about attitude and thinking process. Peebles' funds are as accessible to black architects as to the non-architect minority developers. The burden of capitalizing on this opportunity rests squarely on the shoulder of black architects.

Given Peebles background it is no surprise or accident that of all of the nation's handful of really substantial black developers, Peebles would be the one to do this. He is a native Washingtonian who launched his real estate development career in DC during the 1980s under the Marion Barry administration.

Peebles' rationale for starting his fund, the absence of black access to equity capital, and his broad criteria for the type of firms his firm will capitalize are made to order for the renegade architect-entrepreneur who has been properly acclimated to the rules of capital. Those rules are simple; there must be an industry-standard-acceptable return on the investment, and with reasonable security.

Peebles' $500 million fund could easily leverage an additional one billion dollars in secured debt financing. The resulting $1.5 billion could produce 5,000 housing units, mostly in the affordability range if properly combined with federal, state, and local funding tools.

Peebles' funding initiative could trigger a respectable number of similar initiatives from black as well as white and other non-black sources of equity capital looking to make investments that are financially sound. The tens of billions of dollars in equity funds to match the Peebles initiative could leverage hundreds of billions more. We are now talking about the kind of money that could facil-

9.18 Don Peebles, Jr.
Source: Wikipedia Commons

itate a substantial Black America presence and position in the thing loosely referred to as the Affordable Housing Industry.

Black architects who can be reoriented to the direct pursuit of development finance capital will be providing vital leadership in Black America's move towards collectively building things. This "build one million houses" wing of black architects will rightly complement the other vital wing of black architect who are the designers, story tellers, and high-profile culture producers.

10. New Business Models for Architectural Practice

The Jair Lynch Company

The 45-year-old founder of this now 20-year-old Washington, DC, company is not a licensed or formally trained architect. This founding visionary is an African American who has two Stanford University degrees—a B.S. in civil engineering and a B.A. in urban design. He is also a Harvard Loeb Fellow. His father, a retired college professor, was a prominent activist in the national Black Power movement of the 1960s–1980s era. The following are excerpts from the mission statement on the Jair Lynch Company website:

> Jair Lynch Real Estate Partners specializes in the responsible transformation of walkable urban places. We do this by combining social responsibility with sound economic development in pursuit of creating sustainable, extraordinary neighborhoods that connect to the soul of a place. Our goal is to be a catalyst for transforming neighborhoods that will create value for our stakeholders... Founded in 1998, we have developed over 4.2 million square feet of real estate projects valued at over $1 billion and have almost 1.8 million sf of development in progress valued at more than $750 million....Our projects have been recognized with national and regional awards, including honors from the AIA and the Royal Institute of British Architects.

Recently in Washington, DC, there was a credible story circulating about Lynch's company having received a fresh new $200 million housing funding commitment from one of the most wealthy and powerful institutional investors in the nation. Lynch announced that the housing he intended to develop from this fund would all be affordable and workforce targeted. Lynch has the proven know-how and credibility to actually do that.

Technically, $200 million could be used as the front-end site acquisition and predevelopment money amount required to leverage an additional $800 million from conventional bank-type sources of construction loan funds. That may or may not be what Lynch and his big institutional partner money source have planned. But that is a common and doable scenario.

The Harvard Graduate School of Design (HGSD) is consistently ranked as one of the most influential architecture schools in the world. My speculation is that a facsimile of Jair Lynch's mission statement will inevitably be adopted and promoted by the HGSD as the rightful goal for HGSD architecture graduates desiring to pursue entrepreneurial practices. HGSD training of designers of signature, stand-alone, non-residential structures for wealthy patrons (public or private) will continue for students with those types of career aspirations. But it is inevitable that HGSD will use its considerable influence to advance the idea of the architect as an entrepreneur who should be in full control of the building enterprise. "Design" purists can take heart in knowing that HGSD will boldly assert "better control of design" as the justification for the creation of a new "architect-entrepreneur" curriculum track offered at the global pinnacle of architectural education.

Other architecture programs–typified by Woodbury University in Southern California and the New School in San Diego–have already developed professional graduate programs designed to produce architect-entrepreneurs. Their faculties explicitly seek to produce licensed architects who will start companies structured to do precisely what Jair Lynch does, though usually (though not limited to) a smaller scale. Architect-developer Jonathan Segal, a Woodbury faculty member, is the prototype twenty-first century practitioner who is rapidly coming to be the model for the typical graduate of those types of architecture programs.

For a host of reasons that could fill up another book, African American architect-practitioners cannot look to any established black real estate developers (or any other developers as a rule) as a source of fee-for-services design contracts. The black architect's only option for becoming a serious and measurable factor in meeting the housing needs of Black America is to directly incorporate at least some facsimile of the Jair Lynch business model as their own professional practice modus operandi. The scale of those models can range from small to medium to large.

Katerra, Design-Builder/High-tech Construction Operation

In addition to the Jair Lynch Company representative real estate developer model, the Katerra company is the representative model for companies that fully integrate development, design, finance, fabrication, and modular construction. Katerra is a large, majority-owned firm whose founders are from the private-equity investment-banking sector. Katerra brings two big and important insights to the table. The first is that there is a long overdue need for a revolu-

10.1. Katerra automated, fabrication-modularized plant, Phoenix AR. ca. 2018:
Source: Wikipedia Commons

tion in the nation's construction industry, particularly the building construction sector. Katerra is moving to make the revolution happen. Katerra's vehicle is the affordable housing crisis. Katerra objective is to capture market share by delivering lower hard construction costs and drastically shortening the time of project deliveries.

> *"Our unique "Integrated Factory" model connects Katerra facto-ries directly to our job sites, ensuring a seamless transition from manufacturing, through delivery and installation. This approach extends the speed, precision, coordination, and quality assur-ance of our factory environments directly to Katerra job sites."*
> ***www.katerra.com***

Katerra's other big insight is their educated calculation that levels of return on capital from pursuing that first insight can be large enough to attract equity in-vestment capital from lesser known as well as institutional sources. To produce ar-chitects who will routinely found or co-found Katerra-type firms requires restruc-turing the current architecture school curricula in order to produce much greater levels of understanding of development finance and supply chain technology.

Those are skills that are as teachable and learnable as the skills of conventional design of buildings. The housing arena is an ideal avenue. Katerra (and Kater-ra-like companies) is in reality an "at-risk construction manager," also known as a "design–builder" operation taken to a logical conclusion. Companies with pre-cisely these business-model variations are inexorably obliterating the orthodox fee-for-services model that undergirds the professional practice of architecture. A new breed, next generation of licensed architects as well as existing ortho-dox architectural practitioners must carefully heed Katerra's own words about its thoughtfully chosen target market of affordable housing:

> And the housing shortage is a challenge that we must meet. In 2016, the United States was short more than 7 million affordable and available rental unit apartments... Optimizing architecture and construction [with development finance capital] can get us there. . .. The next step is to integrate design directly with man-ufacturing and the supply chain... Such integration provides the opportunity to aggregate demand for building materials, creat-ing cost savings across multiple projects.

Katerra is now a several-billion-dollar company whose business model can be emulated. The encouraging news is that the current multi-billion-dollar Katerra model is also workable at smaller scales of between $10 million to $100 million. A Katerra business model is also doable at the $1 million to $10 million scale. Those are not difficult amounts of investment capital to raise by properly trained and motivated African American architect–entrepreneurs who align themselves with the right type of interdisciplinary partnerships.

Women Architect Leadership Models

Consistent with other trends of this era, the leadership of African American architects in their necessary reinvention of themselves over the coming decade will come largely from the ascendency of African American women in architecture. We must be ever mindful that *time* has been unfolding at a geometric, rather than an arithmetic, rate. The information revolution has unleashed the capacity to traverse a fifty-year span of cultural change over the next five years or less.

10.2 Kimberly Dowdell.
Source: Wikipedia Commons

Consider that it was nearly fifty years ago when a dozen African American male practitioners founded the National Organization of Minority Architects (NOMA). The founders had a limited objective that fit those times. The organization sought to be a counterpart to the American Institute of Architects (AIA) while also breaking down the doors to local and federal government agencies charged with letting contracts to design publicly financed buildings.

Concurrently, black protest—sometimes violent—led to the direct black political power required to achieve some measure of the limited NOMA objective. Today's NOMA—now with one thousand dues-paying members, nearly one-third females—just elected its fourth woman president.

Kimberly Dowdell is the first NOMA president who pointedly brands herself as an *architect, developer, and educator.* Dowdell is a licensed architect and adjunct architecture professor at the University of Michigan. In May 2019, Dowdell joined the Chicago office of HOK in the role of principal and director of business development. HOK is one of the ten largest architectural firms in the country. She joins a very small number of other black females who are principals in top ten nationally ranked architecture firms. Chicago, a world class city and center for architecture and development, recently elected an African American female mayor. This should be a valuable asset to Dowdell.

Prior to HOK Dowell was a partner in Detroit-based Century Partners, a racially, ethnically, and discipline-diverse company. Century Partners has a vision and mission statement that is an unmistakably compressed version of the Jair Lynch vision and mission statement:

> Our mission is to facilitate holistic revitalization through sustainable residential housing development that embraces grassroots community outreach and the power of creative place-making.

Century's mission statement practically assures that the company could approach and possibly exceed Jair Lynch's current goal of raising millions in investment capital to develop thousands of affordable housing units.

Dowdell's past leadership in Century Partners, her new role at HOK in Chicago, and her presidency at NOMA provide her with a platform to facilitate new think-

10.3 Pascale Sablan. Source: Courtesy of Pascale Sablan.

ing and acting by the coming generation of African American architects.

NOMA's paradigm-shifting female leadership extends beyond just Kim Dowdell as president. A second female is bringing to NOMA a state-of-the-art level of sophisticated and effective communications. Pascale Sablan, a New York licensed architect, who at the time of her initial licensure was number 315 on the list of living black licensed women in the United States to achieve that distinction. She has been an award-winning designer since graduating from Columbia's architecture master's program. She earned her undergraduate degree from Pratt Institute.

Sablan has been able to apply her talents to high-profile projects around the globe. Sablan has a decade of NOMA service. She is currently the NOMA northeast regional vice president and a very viable prospect as a future NOMA president as well as an AIA president. She is also a NOMA national board member and serves as the official NOMA historian. From those perches, Sablan is pushing communications initiatives originally undertaken by past NOMA leadership to a whole new level. NOMA, under the leadership of Dowdell and Sablan, is a critically required element in moving architects of all races, genders, and persuasions to true national leadership.

The Diaspora Space Revisited

The contrasts between what I experienced in Ghana in 1999 and in present-day West and South Africa just two decades later are striking in regards to Ghana's architects and the nation's urbanized development. Ghana is a very good example of much of the sub-Saharan continent. The African states all acknowledge their destinies as urban nations. They are nearly unanimous in their intent to transform the European cities left to them by their former colonial masters. The vision is distinctly African urbanization, but there appears to be universal agreement of the need to adopt the best practices of American and European cities that are transforming into "smart cities."

In May 2017, the Central African nation of Rwanda created and released the document "Smart Sustainable Cities: A Blueprint for Africa" that is highly representative of an "African urban agenda." The full acceptance of the proposition that cities, through cutting-edge science and technology, are "engines of (national) growth" is a reality. The current and emerging generation of African architects seem to embrace that proposition, though with a distinctly African history and culture overlay. Capital investments and technical assistance provided by China and other Asian nations are also important to the positive urbanization of West African nations. The role of agriculture in African nations will be transformed by science and technology in much the same ways as it has in the advanced developed nations in the West and Asia.

10.4. Accra Ghana skyline ca. 2018. Source: Wikipedia Commons

Current and emerging African American architects who aspire to founding twenty-first century entrepreneurial professional practices can now enlarge their lens of opportunities to include sub-Saharan Africa. In fact, their viability may require that they do so. But those opportunities cannot come through arcane theories or superficial twentieth century notions about architecture. African American architects must go to Africa as *partners* bringing investment capital along with vision and a willingness to learn from their African architect-counterparts and business partners. Looking at Ghana and other cities in western and southern Africa, one will see unlimited opportunities.

Rapidly urbanizing African cities welcome African American architects, *but not as fee for services building designers*. The need is for African American architects as risk-taking investors with vision, capital, and a passion for capitalizing on basic marketplace needs in housing, infrastructure, and other related economic-development arenas of national priority. In turn, African American architects need urban Africa as a part of the solution that African American and African architects must both seek out in their attempts to reconstruct a meaningful African American and African architecture for the twenty-first century.

In 2000, a year after returning to Washington, DC from Africa, I attended an all-day symposium, "Defining African Architecture," in the auditorium of the University of Maryland School of Architecture, at College Park. This symposium was organized and presided over by Paul Taylor, an African American architect and Morgan State professor at that time.

There were four main presenters: Mr. W. Enninful-Eghan, a senior lecturer in the Department of Architecture at the University of Science and Technology, Kumasi, Ghana; Ms. Abimbola Asojo, a Nigerian native who was trained in London, as well as at Awolowo at Ile-Ife in Nigeria, and is currently associate dean and professor of interior design in the College of Design, University of Minnesota; Dr. Nnamdi Elleh, a Nigerian native and a researcher at Northwestern University at Evanston, Illinois. Elleh is the author of *African Architecture: Evolution and Transformation (1997)*; and Jack Travis, the New York City architect and leading practitioner-architect of the consciously and unapologetically "black (or African American) architecture" idea. Travis is also the author of *African American Architects in Current Practice (1991)*. Mr. W. Enninful-Eghan's conference-opening keynote address stated that:

> "African architecture is in crisis. It is in crisis because it is not developing with a definite character that is authentically African."

I felt then in 2000 that the issue was far more complex than the issue of authenticity. I have traveled back to West (and Southern) Africa several times since my initial visit. I have made numerous African architect friends and colleagues since then who continue to live, practice, and teach in Africa. Several of those men and women are former students of mine who studied and acquired professional degrees (and became licensed) in America.

I was able to return to Africa as an invited lecturer on the topics I had raised in my 2002 book, *The Crisis of the African American Architect*. On those occasions I began seeing a new generation of young African architect-practitioners who are deeply engaged in debate about the role of the architect in contrast with the post–World War II modernist role grafted onto their countries by former European colonial powers.

Sub-Saharan architects still largely follow the same paradigms of educational and professional practice found in America and Great Britain. However, changes are happening that are very similar to those occurring in the American and British schools and practices. The issue of finding an authentic African architecture has broadened since 2000 to include environmentalism, indigenous natural materials, renewable energy, climate impact, homelessness, and socioeconomic and gender equity. African architects are reacting and adapting to the information technology revolution, as have their American and European counterparts. While belated, the adjustments are occurring at the same exponentially accelerating rates.

10.5 Joe Osae-Addo.
Source: Wikipedia Commons

No discourse about today's African architect scene would be complete without looking at the life and contributions of Joe Osae-Addo. The sixty-year-old Ghanaian was born in Accra and studied at the Architectural Association (AA) in London (1980–1986). He has worked for architectural firms in Finland, the United Kingdom, and the United States. He exerts enormous influence through his role as chairman of the nearly twenty-year-old ArchiAfrika.

He maintains offices in Accra and Tamale in Ghana, Washington, DC, and Los Angeles, California. He lived and practiced in Los Angeles for sixteen years. His current firm, Constructs, LLC, synergizes architec-

10.6. Nana Akua Birmeh. (front row, center, vermillion colored dress) and her ARCHXENUS staff office photo, ca. 2017. Source: Wikipedia Commons

ture, urban planning, landscaping, and building technology into a single unit geared toward using modern architecture and building techniques to create innovative design solutions to contemporary African architecture. His firm is a vigorous advocate for solutions of "smart" and "indigenous" development.

Today I am seeing the presence of a critical mass of new African architects who can offer a great deal to their African American counterparts. These young African architects, similar to their most savvy young, white, Asian, and Hispanic American

10.7 Guillaume Koffi and Issa Diabaté. Source: Wikipedia Commons

architect counterparts, are exploring boundary-breaking methods of practice that provide them with more control over design and other critical decision-making.

Currently in Ghana, the awakening in sound and appropriate architectural practice is exemplified by a decade-old practice founded by Ghana-trained architect, Nana Akua Birmeh. The collective faces of her now forty-person practice speaks volumes. Birmeh's staff of architects, technologists, construction managers, and administrators is led by mostly females. The practice culture is literally structured around the needs of child-bearing and child-rearing young African women architects.

Just 225 miles west of Accra, Ghana in the coastal city of Abidjan, Cote d'Ivoire the architectural firm Koffi & Diabaté is another African model that African American architects can learn from. This nation of 23 million people is a former French colony but had been part of the Ghana Empire before colonization. The nation's growing middle class and educated elites are also English speakers who are highly westernized.

In 2001, Guillaume Koffi, a Paris-trained Ivory Coast architect with over thirty years of experience in the design and management of major projects in Africa, joined forces with American trained Ivorian architect Issa Diabaté. In 2012, the two partners formed the Koffi & Diabaté Group, a broadly integrated practice that specializes in architecture, real estate development and construction.

Diabaté holds a master in architecture degree from Yale. From 1991 to 1993, Issa Diabaté interned in architecture firms in Côte d'Ivoire, in the United States in the Washington, DC office of Devrouax and Purnell, and in France in the offices of Jean Nouvel.

10.8 Les Residence Chocolat Acoco. Source: Wikipedia Commons

Currently Diabaté is developing the first independent architecture school in Abidjan, the capital city of Côte d' Ivoire. He is embarking on the creation of the next generation of Ivorian architects who will be equipped to help his nation move to true independence.

Les Residence Chocolat Acoco is a large-scale project that the firm is developing and designing in partnership with the Ivorian government. The new project encompasses massive restoration of deteriorated areas and the creation of a new drainage system as well as new luxury urban mixed-use redevelopment. The partners believe that projects like Chocolat Residences Acoco are necessary to provide examples of quality urban planning by Ivorian professionals that can be emulated throughout the nation.

Concluding Thoughts

The word *architecture* implies a false neutrality and innocence. In architecture the success or failure of things are based on visual sensibilities as measured by a self-anointed high priesthood. *Group* economics are outside of the bounds of acceptable architectural discourse. In this book I have been talking about architecture but not really talking about architecture.

Meanwhile the Information Age Revolution is providing us with the capacity to make credible guesses about most material things that are going to happen in the United States over the next decade. Those guesses assume the absence of the occurrence of existential events like nuclear war or reaching the tipping point of catastrophic atmospheric carbon overload.

We can predict that over the next decade in the United States, population increases plus unmet needs will necessitate the building of millions of new housing units. Those housing units will also require new ancillary commercial-civic spaces and a robust civil infrastructure. Nearly all of this growth will be in cities and surrounding metropolitan areas. An increasing amount of this building will happen through a rapid integration of many things into a seamless whole. This constitutes a revolution in construction. To participate at a meaningful level requires revolutionary levels of changes in behavior and attitude.

There is a raging national housing crisis that is literally destroying Black America's prospects for maintaining cohesive and viable urban community presences. The National Urban League 2017 State of Black America Report's theme and call for an urban main street Marshall Plan may no longer be just a pipe dream. The burning question is who will be the actual builders of the parts of the Plan that will be presumptively aimed at reversing the negative tides of gentrification in Black America's urban communities?

Today's African American (and African) architects as designers and storytellers—exemplified by the brilliant NMAAHC architects—are a vital necessity but nowhere near sufficient. There is an equally important need for a new generation of architects as "urban community builders." Both wings must join forces with Black America's political, cultural, and business leadership in pushing for a new Marshall Plan-scale urban economic redevelopment in Black America's city-centered beachheads. Those hard-won lands are being lost at an accelerating pace to massively disruptive gentrification.

Black America presently contains a loose assortment of relatively anemic entities that can be vaguely seen as a nascent "building industry." The entities include financial institutions, real estate brokers, building contractors, subcontractors, fabricators, equipment and materials suppliers, title companies, law firms, architects, real estate developers, skilled trades persons, property managers, unskilled laborers, and an assortment of grassroots entrepreneurs.

If Marshall Plan-type funds and resources materialize and Black America fails to come together and control rebuilding in those urban communities, others will. For example, imagine China's financial situation today had that nation not demanded twenty-five years ago the right to totally control and execute the development of their physical environment in exchange for American businesses being granted access to China's markets and labor.

As things now stand, the end result of the physical redevelopment of urban spaces currently still occupied by black Americans will actually be a linear continuation of the redevelopment of America's cities that began in 1968. Such an outcome at the end of one or two decades hence are inevitable without a radical change today in how and who will control and execute the actual redevelopment in urban Black America.

Today, with the benefit of hindsight, we can clearly see two past eras of Black Reconstruction in America. The first one started in 1866 and within twelve years was terminated with extreme violence. The second era began a century later in 1968 upon the death of Dr. Martin Luther King, Jr. The next several years in this nation's electoral cycle will determine whether this second reconstruction era in America shall continue moving forward or continue to regress. In either case, things over the coming decade will be happening in the face of global-scale technological, financial, and climate-related disruptions to everything.

Regarding black businesses, the prospect of having black information-age moguls is currently well along in the first quarter of the twenty-first century. Evidence abounds that the black moguls derive the base—not to be confused with the entirety—of their fortunes from Black America or black diaspora markets. Robert Johnson was the first African American to achieve billionaire status. He made his initial fortune through catering exclusively to the needs, longings, desires, and cultural predilections of Black America. Johnson expanded his black-oriented offerings and services to the white (or "crossover") market. But Johnson was always respectful of his black base. He proceeded without sentiment from an awareness that he had to hold his base while moving to the next level. Johnson knew that this is the nature of how all successful businesses are built: *from a firm base!*

Despite a tumultuous "love-hate" relationship (due to programming choices made by Johnson's Black Entertainment Television network), Johnson and Black America were always *culturally fused*. Johnson shared this fusion with the crop of brilliant young black filmmakers that were headed initially in the 1990s by Spike Lee and John Singleton (and preceded by Oscar Michaux of the 1920s). These men did not bring or attempt to impose an alien culture of fundamentally differing tastes and styles on Black America. Despite Johnson's Ivy League education in high finance and Lee's New York University education in filmmaking (with an undergraduate degree from HBCU Morehouse in Atlanta), they remained *of* Black America.

Johnson's BET network was built on meeting the needs, one-on-one and one by one, of millions of black households—black customers, if you will. Fortunately for today's Bob Johnsons, now succeeded by the Oprah Winfreys and Tyler Perrys, they are not faced with a white America of the same mentality that confronted Booker T. Washington or W.E.B. DuBois one hundred years ago.

The next generation of African American architects—like Johnson, Winfrey,

Perry, and many other radio, film, TV, entertainment, and telecommunications entrepreneurs—must be made to see the tens of millions of *customers* in black lower- and middle-class America (in contradiction to the "patrons and clients" obsession fostered by architecture culture orthodoxy). These customers are eager to spend their dollars with other black people who offer first-class services while knowing and respecting them on the most fundamental level of culture, aesthetics, spirituality, and economic imperatives in a pluralist nation of competing *groups*.

We began this book's PART III, "Realigning Architecture with the Black Agenda (2020-2030)," with a pithy quote about the relationship between architecture and money. *It's always about the money.* Better stated, *it's always about the intersection of money, behavior, attitude, perceptions, culture, power, and action.* African American architects today are at a "cast down your buckets" moment in history. In that metaphor the "sea" is the perennial cities-based affordable housing crisis and Black America's imperative for immediate direct and focused *group* action on its own behalf.

Today's National Organization of Minority Architects (NOMA) can become a prime force vehicle for the movement needed to begin immediately building a Black America-controlled affordable housing industry. But NOMA must become as politically effective as its American Institute of Architects (AIA) counterpart. In the matter of aiding Black America's Black Agenda and the quest to immediately build a functioning affordable housing industry, NOMA's national body and local chapters are well positioned. NOMA must become a major facilitator of access to public and private capital (money) for current and prospective licensed architects who prioritize the development/design/building of houses and community development. Those architects are in the real estate business as well as in the construction business. Both are rapidly morphing into high-tech enterprises. A high-tech label translates to "bankability." Lenders and investors are just asking for a "business plan" that includes hard collateral assets like land, houses and small apartment buildings...*and lender/investors will fund the acquisition of those things if appropriately packaged.*

NOMA's affiliation with the national AIA (and concomitant co-dependency) has reached a point of diminishing returns. There must now be a sharp pivot. NOMA, through its sprawling network of local professional and university-based student chapters, must make structural common cause with key organizations in Black America. The priority targets must be the young but rapidly growing Buy the Block movement of grassroots activists, the local chapters of African American real estate professionals and realtors, and local chapters of the National Urban League. Overriding all of those alliances must be the ones with this nation's progressive political movements and progressive congressional figures now moving legislation on reversing the destruction of the environment, creating a green economy, and the massive re-invention of social/public housing.

Out of such alliances will come the birth of a truly new socio-economic and culturally just architecture and planning movement that could, over the next decade, reverse the past fifty-years of accelerating destruction of urban Black America.

Acknowledgments

In this sequel to my 2002 book *The Crisis of the African Architect* I continue my use of mainly secondary sources in support of my speculations about the twentieth-century evolution of African American architects. I continue to draw upon on three currently obscure and unpublished doctoral dissertations, one by Richard Kevin Dozier, now a retired professor and dean of the Robert Taylor School of Architecture at Tuskegee University in Tuskegee, Alabama (he was highly instrumental in creating the Robert Taylor School of Architecture). Dr. Dozier's professional life-long odyssey of scholarly research has unearthed countless precious details about the origin of today's African American architects and predecessor black building craftsmen dating back to the 1600s.

The second dissertation is by the late Washington, DC historian Harrison Etheridge who completed his work in 1979. Etheridge delved deep into the follow-up role of Howard University in architectural education from the early 1920s to the beginning of the 1970s. He gave me an early draft copy of his dissertation in 1973 when I was a very a young faculty member in the School of Architecture at Howard University.

The third dissertation, completed in 1992 by retired architecture professor Wesley Henderson, is on the life and times of Los Angeles-based architects Paul R. Williams, the most celebrated African American architect in the twentieth-century, and James H. Garrott, a still obscure but pivotal black avant-garde modernist of the 1940s era. Having grown up in Los Angeles between 1946 and 1961, I have a particular appreciation for the breadth, depth, and richness of Dr. Henderson's research.

The dissertations provide irrefutable evidence of a triangular-shaped connection between Tuskegee, Alabama, Washington, DC, and the city of Los Angeles in the twentieth century evolution of African American architects.

I continue my indebtedness to Washington, DC, landscape architect Dreck Wilson for his reading of the manuscript and many helpful observations. His seminal 2004 published book, *African American Architects: A Biographical Dictionary, 1865-1945* is the indispensable work for anyone attempting to write on the subject. Wilson's most recent book, *Julian Abele, Architect and the Beaux Arts (2019)* was also an important source. I am also indebted to Brad Grant, a long-time colleague who is a professor in the Howard University Department of Architecture. His reading of several succeeding draft manuscripts of this book and pointed critiques have been priceless. However, none of the above persons bears any responsibility for this final document. Any errors or inaccuracies are mine alone.

I am also indebted to the students that I taught or mentored between February 2016 and May 2018, my two years at Howard as the James Silcott Professor of Architecture. The Howard University students were one of my biggest motivations for completing this book. Many of them will be the next generation of African American (and other) design and planning professionals. Hopefully, they will practice their professions in ways that acknowledge and celebrate African American culture and its actual contributions to American architecture, landscape architecture, and city planning while fully appreciating the importance of their own agency in what they can accomplish.

Bibliography

Black Architects & Architecture

Adjaye, David and Allison, Peter (Editor). New York. *Adjaye African Architecture*. Thames & Hudson, 2016

Anderson, Genell, *The Call of the Ancetors*. Washington, DC: AMAR, 1991.

Bird, Betty and Schwartz, Nancy, *Thematic Study of Black Architects, Builders, and Developers in Washington, DC*. Washington, DC: United Planning Organization, 1993.

Bond, Max Jr, "Still Here; Three Afro-American Architects: Julian F. Abele, Hilyard Robinson, and Paul R. Williams." *Harvard Design Magazine*, summer 1997, Cambridge.

Cheney, Ruth Helen, "Advocacy Planning; What It Is, And How It Works." *Progressive Architecture*. September 1968

Dozier, Richard Kevin, "Tuskegee: Booker T. Washington's Contribution to the Education of Black Architects." A Doctoral Dissertation—University of Michigan, 1990.

Etheridge, Harrison, "Black Architects of Washington, DC: 1900 to the Present." A Doctoral Dissertation, The Catholic University, Washington, DC, 1979.

Elleh, Nnamdi, *African Architecture: Evolution and Transformation*. New York: McGraw-Hill, 1997.

Fields, Daryl W; Fuller, Kevin L; and Curry, Milton S.F. (Ed.), *APPEN- DIX (Issues 1,2, & 3) Culture, Theory, Praxis*. Cambridge, Mass: Appendix Inc., 1993, 1994, & 1996.

Fields, Daryl W, "Architecture and the Black Subject: An Ethno-Historic Reconstruction." A Doctoral Dissertation, Harvard Graduate School of Design, 1995.

Fry, E. Louis Sr., "Louis Edwin Fry, Sr: His Life and His Architecture." An Unpublished Autobiography, Wash., DC, 1986.

Gooden, Mario, *Dark Space. Architecture Representation Black Identity*. New York: Columbia Books on Architecture and the City, 2016

Gradison, Kenrick Ian, "From Plantation to Campus: Progress, Community, and the Lay of the Land in Shaping the Early Tuskegee Campus." *Landscape Journal*, Volume 15, Number 1, spring 1996.

Henderson, Wesley Howard, "Two Case Studies of African-American Architects' Careers in Los Angeles: 1890-1945, Paul R. Williams, FAIA and James Garrott, AIA." A Doctoral Dissertation, Univ. of Calif. at Los Angeles, 1992.

Hudson, Karen, *Paul R. Williams Architect: A Legacy of Style*. New York: Rizzoli, 1994.

Hughes, David, *Afrocentric Architecture: A Design Primer*. Columbus, OH: Greyden Press, 1994.

Moody, Curtis J., *MOODY NOLAN DESIGN*. Columbus, OH: Moody Nolan Inc., 2013.

Robinson, Harry G, FAIA and Edwards, Ruth Hazel, Ph.D., *The Long Walk: Place Making At Howard University*. Washington, DC: Moorland-Spingarn Research Center, 1998.

Travis, Jack (Ed.), *African-American Architects in Current Practice.* New York: Princeton Architectural Press, 1991.

Weiss, Ellen, Robert R. Taylor and Tuskegee: *An African American Architect Designs for Booker T. Washington.* Montgomery, AL. NewSouth Books, 2012.

Wilson, Dreck (Ed.), *African-American Architects: A Biographical Dictionary 1865-1945.* New York London ROUTLEDGE, 2004.

Wilson, Mabel O., *Negro Building: Black Americans in the World of Fairs and Museums.* Berkeley Los Angeles London: University of California Press, 2012

Wilson, Mabel O., *Begin With The Past: Building the National Museum of African American History and Culture.* Washington, DC: Smithsonian Books, 2016

Vlach, John Michael, *Back of the Big House: The Architecture of Plantation Slavery.* Chapel Hill: University of North Carolina Press, 1993.

The Afro-American Tradition in Decorative Arts. Athens, GA.: Brown Thrasher Books, 1990.

Black Art, Music, & Culture

Algotsson, Sharne and Davis, Denys, *The Spirit of African Design.* New York: Clarkson Potter Publishers, 1996.

Appiah, Kwame Anthony, *In My Father's House: Africa In The Philosophy of Culture.* New York: Oxford University Press, 1992.

Appiah, Kwame Anthony and Gates, Henry Louis, *Africana: The Encyclopedia of the African and African-American Experience.* New York: Basic Civitas Books, 1999.

Bearden, Romare and Henderson, Harry, *A History of African-American Artists From 1792 to the Present.* New York: Pantheon Books, 1993.

Benjamin, Tritobia Hayes, *The Life and Art of Lois Mailou Jones.* San Francisco: Pomegranate Art books, 1994.

Bernal, Martin, *Black Athena: The Afroasiatic Roots of Classical Civilization, Vol. I & II.* New Brunswick: Rutgers University Press, 1987, 1991.

Crouch, Stanley, *Always in Pursuit. Fresh Perspectives.* New York, Vintage Books, 1998.

Ellington, Edward Kennedy, *Music Is My Mistress.* New York: Da Capo Press, 1973.

George, Nelson, *Hip-Hop America.* New York: Viking, 1998.

Gioia, Ted, *The History of Jazz.* New York: Oxford University Press, 1997.

Harris, Leonard, *The Critical Pragmatism of Alain Locke: A Reader in Value Theory, Aesthetics, Community, Culture, Race, and Education.* Lanham, MD: Rowman & Littlefield Publishers, Inc., 1999.

Hooks, bell, *Art on My Mind: Visual Politics.* New York: The New Press, 1995.

Howe, Steven, *Afrocentrism: Mythical Pasts and Imagined Homes.* London: VERSO, 1998.

Karenga, Maulana, *Introduction To Black Studies.* Los Angeles: University of Sankore Press, 1991.

Kelley, Robin D.G., *Yo' Mama's DisfunKtional!: Fighting the Culture Wars in America.* Boston: Beacon Press, 1997.

Kelley, Norman and Baldwin, Davarian, "Rhythm Nation: The Political Economy of Black Music." *Black Renaissance/Renaissance Noire.* New York, Vol. 2, No. 2, summer 1999, 8-21.

Kirschke, Amy Helene, *Aaron Douglas: Art, Race, & The Harlem Renaissance.* Jackson, MS.: University Press of Mississippi, 1995.

Lefkowitz, Mary R. and Rogers, Guy MacLean, *Black Athena Revisited.* Chapel Hill: University of North Carolina Press, 1996.

Lerner, Michael and West, Cornel, *Jews & Blacks: Let the Healing Begin.* New York: G.P. Putnam's Sons, 1995.

Lewis, Samelia, *African-American Art and Artists.* Berkeley: University of California Press, 1990.

Locke, Alain (Ed.), *The New Negro: Voices of the Harlem Renaissance.* New York: Touchstone, 1997.

Lubiano, Wahneema (Ed.), *The House That Race Built: Original Essays By Toni Morrison, Angela Davis, Cornel West, and Others On Black Americans and Politics in America Today.* New York: Vintage Books, 1998.

Murray, Albert, *The Omni-Americans: Black Experience and American Culture.* New York: Da Capo Press, 1970.

O'Meally, Robert G. (Ed.), *The Jazz Cadence of American Culture.* New York: Columbia University Press, 1998. Patton, Sharon, *African-American Art.* New York: Oxford University Press, 1998.

Peretti, Burton W., *Jazz in American Culture.* Chicago: Ivan R. Dee, 1997.

Powell, Richard J., *Black Art and Culture in the Twentieth-Century.* London: Thames and Hudson, 1997.

Sowell, Thomas, *Race and Culture: A World View.* New York: Basic Books, 1994.

West, Cornel, *The Cornel West Reader.* New York: Basic Civitas Books, 1999.

Willett, Frank, *African Art: An Introduction.* London: Thames and Hudson, 1986.

Black Political History & Theory

Bennett, Lerone Jr, *The Shaping of Black America: The Struggles and Triumphs of Blacks, 1619 to the 1990s.* New York: Penguin Books, 1975.

Brownstein, Elizabeth Smith, *If This House Could Talk: Historic Homes, Extraordinary Americans.* New York: Simon & Shuster, 1999.

Cobb, William Jelani (Ed.), *The Essential Harold Cruse: A Reader.* New York: Palgrave, 2002

Cruse, Harold, *Crisis of the Negro Intellectual: A Historical Analysis of the Failure of Black Leadership.* New York: Quill, 1967.

Carmichael, Stokely and Hamilton, Charles V., *Black Power: The Politics of Liberation.* New York: Vintage Books, 1992.

Franklin, John Hope and Meier, August (Ed.), *Black Leaders of the Twentieth-Century.* Chicago: University of Illinois Press, 1982.

Harland, Lewis, *Booker T. Washington in Perspective.* Jackson, MS.: Univ. of Mississippi Press, 1988.

Logan, Rayford W., *The Betrayal of the Negro: From Rutherford B. Hayes to Woodrow Wilson.* New York: Da Capo Press, 1997.

Marable, Manning, *Black Leadership.* New York: Columbia University Press, 1998.

Meier, August, *Negro Thought In America 1880-1915: Racial Ideologies in the Age of Booker T. Washington.* Ann Arbor, MI: The University of Michigan Press, 1988.

Mosely, Walter (Ed.), *Black Genius: African-American Solutions to African-American Problems.* New York: W.W. Norton & Co., 1999.

Moses, Wilson Jeremiah, *Afrotopia: The Roots of African American Popular History.* Cambridge, UK: Cambridge University Press, 1998

Robinson, Randall, *The Debt: What America Owes Blacks*. New York: Dutton, 2000.

Rydell, Robert (Ed.), *The Reason Why The Colored American Is Not In The World Columbian Expedition*. Chicago: University of Illinois, 1999.

Steele, Shelby, *The Content of Our Character*. New York: Harper Collins, 1994.

Washington, Booker T., *Up From Slavery*. New York: Bantam, 1963.

Wilson, Amos N., *Blueprint for Black Power: A Moral, Political, and Economic Imperative for the Twenty-First Century*. New York: African World Info Systems, 1998.

Blacks & Business

Bundles, A'Lelia, *On Her Own Ground: The Life and Times of Madam C.J. Walker*. New York: Scribner, 2001.

Dingle, Derek T., *Black Enterprise Titans of the B.E.100s: Black CEO's Who Redefined and Conquered American Business*. New York: John Wiley & Sons Inc., 1999.

Fraser, George C., *Race For Success: The Ten Best Business Opportunities For Blacks In America*. New York: William Morrow, 1998.

Graves, Earl G., *How to Succeed in Business Without Being White*. New York: Harper Collins Publishers, Inc., 1997.

Lewis, Reginald, *Why Should White Guys Have All the Fun?: How Reginald Lewis Created a Billion-Dollar Business Enterprise*. New York: John Wiley & Sons, 1995.

Russell, Dick, *Black Genius: The American Experience*. New York: Carroll & Graf Publishers Inc., 1998.

Walker, Juliet E.K., *The History of Black Business in America: Capitalism, Race, Entrepreneurship*. New York: McMillan Library Reference USA, 1998.

American Architectural History, Theory & Politics

Andrews, Wayne, *Architecture, Ambition and Americans: A Social History of American Architecture*. New York: The Free Press, 1964.

Bonta, Juan Pablo, *American Architects and Texts: A Computer-Aided Analysis of the Literature*. Cambridge, MA: The MIT Press, 1996.

Boyer, Ernest L. and Mitgang, Lee D., *Building Community: A New Future For Architecture Education and Practice*. Princeton, NJ: The Carnegie Foundation for the Advancement of Teaching, 1996.

Cramer, James (Ed.), *Almanac of Architecture & Design*. Norcross, GA: Greenway Group, 2000.

Cosbie, Michael, "A White Gentleman's Profession?" *Progressive Architecture*, November 1994.

Caragonne, Alexander, *The Texas Rangers: Notes From an Architectural Underground*. Cambridge, MA: The MIT Press, 1994.

DeSoto, Hernando, *The Mystery of Capital: Why Capitalism Triumphs in the West and Fails Elsewhere*. New York: Basic Books, 2000.

Ellis, Joseph J., *American Sphinx: The Character of Thomas Jefferson*. New York: Vintage Books, 1998.

Edwards, John (Ed.), *Guide to Architecture Schools: Sixth Edition*. Washington, DC: Association of Collegiate Schools of Architecture, 1998.

Eisenman, Peter; Graves, Michael; Gwathmey; Hejduk, John; and Meier, Richard. *Five Architects.* New York: Oxford University Press, 1975.

Frampton, Kenneth, *Studies In Tectonic Culture: The Poetics of Construction in Nineteenth & Twentieth-Century Architecture.* Cambridge, MA: MIT Press, 1996.

Gill, Brendan, *Many Masks; A Life of Frank Lloyd Wright.* New York: Da Capo Press, 1998.

Goodman, Robert, *After the Planners.* New York: Simon and Schuster, 1971.

Gordon-Reed, *Annette, Thomas Jefferson and Sally Hemings; An American Controversy.* Charlottesville, VA: The University of Virginia Press, 1997.

Gutman, Robert, *Architectural Practice; A Critical View.* Princeton, NJ: Princeton Architectural Press, 1988.

Herrnstein, Richard and Murray, Charles, *The Bell Curve: Intelligence and Class Structure in American Life.* New York: Simon & Schuster, 1994.

Hughes, Robert, *American Visions: The Epic History of Art in America.* New York: Alfred A. Knopf, 1999.

Lamster, Mark (Ed.) *Architecture and Film.* New York: Vinata-Ash Press, 2000.

Leccese, Michael and McCormick, Kathleen (Ed.), *Charter of the New Urbanism: Congress for the New Urbanism.* New York: McGraw- Hill, 2000.

Lemann, Nicholas, The *Big Test: The Secret of History of the American Meritocracy.* New York: Farrar, Straus, & Giroux, 1999.

Merriam, Alan P., *The Anthropology of Music.* Chicago: Northwestern University Press, 1964.

Noble, David F., *America By Design; Science, Technology, and The Rise of Corporate Capitalism.* New York: Oxford University Press, 1977.

Oliver, Richard (Ed.), *The Making of an Architect 1881-1981: Columbia University and the City of New York.* New York: Rizzoli, 1981.

Reich, Robert B., *The Work of Nations: Preparing Ourselves for Twenty- first Century Capitalism.* New York: Vintage Books, 1992.

Roth, Leland M., *A Concise History of American Architecture.* New York: Harper & Row, 1979.

Scully, Vincent, *American Architecture and Urbanism.* New York: Henry Holt and Company, 1988.

Secrest, Meryle, *Frank Lloyd Wright: A Biography.* New York: Harper Collins, 1992.

Stern, Robert A.M., *Pride of Place; Building the American Dream.* Boston: Houghton Mifflin Company, 1986.

Thernstrom, Stephan and Thernstrom, Abigail, *America In Black and White; One Nation, Indivisible.* New York: Touchstone-Simon& Shuster, 1997.

Twombley, Robert, *Power and Style: A Critique of Twentieth-Century American Architecture in the U.S.* New York: Hill and Wang, 1995.

Upton, Dell (Ed.), *America's Architectural Roots: Ethnic Groups That Built America.* Washington, DC: Preservation Press, 1986.

Upton, Dell, *Architecture in the United States.* New York: Oxford University

Williamson, Roxanne Kuter, *American Architects and the Mechanics of Fame.* Austin, TX.: University of Texas Press, 1991.

Wolfe, Tom, *From Bauhaus to Our House.* New York: Farrar Straus Giroux, 1981.

Wiseman, Carter, *Shaping a Nation: Twentieth-century American Architecture and its Makers.* New York: W.W. Norton & Company, 1998.

Wojtowicz, Robert, *Lewis Mumford & American Modernism: Eutopian Theories for Architecture and Urban Planning.* Cambridge, UK: Cambridge University Press, 1996.

General Architectural Thought

Banham, Reyner, *Theory of Design in the First Machine Age.* Cambridge, MA: The MIT Press, 1980.

Blake, Peter, *The Master Builders: Le Corbusier, Mies van Der Rohe, and Frank Lloyd Wright.* New York: W.W. Norton & Company, 1976.

Blau, Eve and Troy, Nancy J. (Ed.), *Architecture and Cubism.* Cambridge, MA: The MIT Press, 1997.

Bolotin, Norman and Laing, Christine, *The Chicago World's Fair of 1893: The World's Columbian Exposition.* Washington, DC: The Preservation Press-National Trust for Historic Preservation, 1992.

Brolin, Brent, *The Failure of Modern Architecture.* London: Studio Vista, 1976.

Brosterman, Norman, *Inventing Kindergarten.* New York: Harry Abrams, Inc., 1997.

Chipp, Herschel B., *Theories of Modern Art: A Source Book By Artists and Critics.* Berkeley, CA: University of California Press, 1968.

Cuff, Dana, *Architecture: The Story of Practice.* Cambridge, MA: The MIT Press, 1996.

Curtis, William J.R., *Modern Architecture Since 1900.* London: Phaidon Press Limited, 3rd Ed., 1996.

Le Corbusier; Ideas and Forms. London: Phaidon Press Limited, 1997, 4th Ed., 1997.

Davis, Howard, *The Culture of Building.* New York: Oxford University Press, 1999.

Ellin, Nan, *Postmodern Urbanism.* New York: Princeton Press, 1999.

Etlin, Richard A., *Frank Lloyd Wright & LeCorbusier: The Romantic Legacy.* New York: Manchester University Press, 1994.

Fisher, Thomas R., *In the Scheme of Things: Alternative Thinking on the Practice of Architecture.* Minneapolis: University of Minnesota Press, 2000.

Giedion, Sigfried, *Space, Time and Architecture: The Growth of a New Tradition.* Cambridge, MA: Harvard University Press, 1971.

Isozaki, Arata, *Japan-ness in Architecture.* Cambridge, MA: The MIT Press, 2006.

Jencks, Charles, *Architecture of the Jumping Universe.* New York: Saint Martin's Press, 1995.

Ecstatic Architecture: The Surprising Link. Great Britain: Academy Editions, John Wiley & Sons, 1999.

Le Corbusier: And the Continual Revolution in Architecture. New York: Monacelli Press, 2000.

Jarzombek, Mark, "Molecules, Money and Design: The Question of Sustainability's Role in Architectural Academe." *Thresholds 14*, MIT Dept. of Architecture & Planning, spring 1997, 32-36.

Lewis, Roger K, *Architect? A Candid Guide to the Profession.* Cambridge, MA: The MIT Press, 1985, 1998, 2013

Newhouse, Elizabeth (Ed.), *Builders: The Marvels of Engineering.* Washington, DC: The National Geographic Society, 1992.

Pelli, Cesar, *Observations For Young Architects.* New York: Monecelli Press, 1999.

Press, Joseph, "Soul-Searching: Reflections From the Ivory Tower." *Journal of Architectural Education.* May 1998, Volume 51, No. 4.

Rand, Ayn, *The Fountainhead.* New York: The Bobbs-Merrill Co., 1943.

Rappaport, Amos, *House Form and Culture.* Englewood Cliffs, NJ: Prentice-Hall, 1969.

Risebero, Bill, *Modern Architecture and Design: An Alternative History.* Cambridge, MA: The MIT Press, 1982.

Rowe, Colin (Edited by Alexander Caragonne), *As I Was Saying:*

Recollections and Miscellaneous Essays. Cambridge, MA: The MIT Press, 1996.

Rowe, Colin and Slutzky, Robert, "Transparency: Literal and Phenomenal." *Perspecta No. 8, 1963, Yale School of Architecture Magazine.* Rudofsky, Bernard, *Architecture Without Architects.* New York: Museum of Modern Art, 1964.

Stevens, Gary, *The Favored Circle: The Social Foundations of Architectural Distinction.* Cambridge, MA: The MIT Press, 1998.

Sutton, Ira, *Western Architecture: From Ancient Greece To the Present.* New York: Thames and Hudson, 1999.

Ten Homes That Changed America: Watch. WTTW Chicago, 2 Apr. 2016, https://interactive.wttw.com/ten/homes/watch#.Xf57upNKiRs

Tournikiotis, Panayotis, *The Historiography of Modern Architecture.* Cambridge, MA: The MIT Press, 1999.

Vitruvius (Translated by M.H. Morgan), *The Ten Books of Architecture.* New York: Dover Publications, 1960.

Venturi, Robert, *Complexities and Contradictions In Architecture.* New York: The Museum of Modern Art, 1966.

The Future of Architecture; Planning, Management & "Drawing"

Barnett, Jonathan and Portman, John, *The Architect As Developer.* New York: McGraw Hill, 1976.

Brynjolfsson, Erik and McAfee, Andrew, *The Second Machine Age: Work, Progress, and Prosperity in a Time of Brilliant Technologies.* New York: W.W. Norton & Company, Inc, 2014.

Burden, Ernest, *Design Simulation: Use of Photographic and Electronic Media in Design Presentation.* New York: Whitney Library of Design, 1985.

Chakrabarti. Vishaan., *A Country of Cities: A Manifesto for an Urban America.* New York: Metropolis Books, 2013.

Ching, Francis D.K. and Juroszek, Steven P., *Design Drawing.* New York: Van Nostrand Reinhold, 1998.

Ching, Francis D.K, *Architecture: Form, Space, & Order.* New York: Van Nostrand Reinhold, 1976.

Dixon, Kathy Denise, Kepthart, Timothy A. and Moody, Karl L., *The Business of Architecture: Your Guide to a Financially Successful Firm.* New York and London, 2018.

Evans, Robin, *Translations From Drawing To Building And Other Essays.* Cambridge: The MIT Press, 1986.

Fisher, Thomas R., *In the Scheme of Things: Alternative Thinking on the Practice of Architecture.* Minneapolis: University of Minnesota Press, 2000.

Futagawa, Yukio (Ed.), *Paul Rudolph.* New York: Architectural Book Publishing, Inc., 1972.

Haviland, David S., (Ed.), *The Architect's Handbook of Professional Practice: Student Edition.* Washington, DC: AIA Press, 1996.

Harrigan, John, and Neel, Paul, *The Executive Architect; Transforming Designers Into Leaders.* New York: John Wiley & Sons Inc., 1996.

Heim, Michael, *Virtual Realism*. New York: Oxford University Press, 1998.

Kurzweil, Ray, *The Age of Spiritual Machines: When Computers Exceed Human Intelligence*. New York: Penguin Group, 1999.

Lockard, William Kirby, *Design Drawing (Revised Edition)*. Menlo Park, CA: Crisp Publications, Inc., 1982.

Maas, Winy and Madrazo, Felix, *Copy Paste: The Badass Architectural Copy Guide*. Rotterdam, The Netherlands: The Why Factory and nai010, 2017.

Mitchell, William J., *The Reconfigured Eye: Visual Truth in the Post-Photographic Era*. Cambridge, MA: The MIT Press, 1993.

City of Bits: Space, Place, and the Infobahn. Cambridge, MA: The MIT Press, 1994.

e-topia: "Urban Life, Jim—But Not As We Know It." Cambridge, MA: The MIT Press, 1999.

McCullough, Malcolm, *Abstracting Craft: The Practiced Digital Hand*. Cambridge, MA: The MIT Press, 1996.

Mehaffy, Michael W.., *Cities Alive: Jane Jacobs, Christopher Alexander,and the Roots of the New Urban Renaissance*. Portland, OR: Sustasis Press, 2017.

O'Mara, Martha, *Strategy and Place: Managing Corporate Real Estate and Facilities for Competitive Advantage*. New York: The Free Press, 1999.

Pawley, Martin, *Theory and Design in the Second Machine Age*. Cambridge, MA: Basil Blackwell Ltd, 1990.

Terminal Architecture. London: Reaktion Press, 1998.

Porter, Tom, *The Architect's Eye: Visualization and Depiction of Space in Architecture*. London: E., and F.N. Spon, 1997.

Rifkin, Jeremy, *The Third Industrial Revolution: How Lateral Power is Transforming Energy,the Economy, and the World*. New York: PALGRAVE MACMILLAN, 2011.

Schwab, Klaus, *The Fourth Industrial Revolution*. New York: Crown Business, 2017.

Shepard, Cassim., *City Makers: The Culture and Craft of Practical Urbanism*. New York:: The Monacelli Press, 2017.

Solomon, Daniel, *Housing and the City: Love Versus Hope*. Atglen, PA: Shiffer Publishing, Ltd, 2018.

Washington, DC

Barras, Jonetta Rose, *The Last of the Black Emperors: The Hollow Comeback of Marion Barry in the New Age of Black Leadership*. Baltimore: Bancroft Press, 1998.

Bushong, William; Robinson, Judith Helm, and Mueller, Julie, *A Centennial History of the Washington, DC, Chapter: The American Institute of Architects—1887-1987*. Washington, DC: The Washington Architectural Foundation Press, 1978.

Jaffe, Harry and Sherwood, Tom, *Dream City: Race, Power, and the Decline of Washington DC*. New York: Simon & Schuster, 1994.

Gillette, Howard Jr., *Between Justice and Beauty; Race, Planning, And the Failure of Urban Policy in Washington, DC*. Baltimore: The Johns Hopkins University Press, 1995.

Asch, Chris Myers and Musgrove, George Derek, *Chocolate City: A History of Race and Democracy in the Nation's Capital*. Chapel Hill, NC: The University of North Carolina Press, 2017.

Siegal, Fred, *The Future Once Happened Here: New York, DC, LA, and the Fate of America's Big Cities*. New York: The Free Press, 1997.

Tennenbaum, Robert, *Creating a New City: Columbia, Maryland*. Columbia, MD: Partners in Community Building and Perry Publishing, 1990.

Van Dyne, Larry, "The Making of Washington—Men of Vision and Ambition Who Built a Great City and Made Great Fortunes." *Washingtonian Magazine*, September 1997, Volume 23, No. 2.

Index

Made in the USA
Columbia, SC
15 December 2021

51600835R00108